EDUCATIONAL PHILOSOPHY
Foundations and Philosophers

Custom Edition for The University of Missouri-St. Louis

With Material From

Philosophical and Ideological Perspectives on Education, Second Edition
by Gerald L. Gutek

Philosophical Documents in Education, Second Edition
by Ronald F. Reed and Tony W. Johnson

Excerpts taken from:

Philosophical and Ideological Perspectives on Education, Second Edition
by Gerald L. Gutek
Copyright © 1997, 1988 by Allyn & Bacon
A Pearson Education Company
Boston, Massachusetts 02116

Printed in the United States of America

10 9 8 7 6 5 4 3 2 1

Please visit our web site at www.pearsoncustom.com

ISBN 0–536–67753–0

BA 994255

PEARSON CUSTOM PUBLISHING
75 Arlington Street, Suite 300, Boston, MA 02116
A Pearson Education Company

Contents

Chapter 1

Essentialism and Education

Essentialism is a theory that asserts that education properly involves the learning of the basic skills, arts, and sciences that have been useful in the past and are likely to remain useful in the future. The Essentialist, as the name suggests, believes that there are some essential, or basic, skills that have contributed to human well-being, such as reading, writing, arithmetic, and civilized social behavior that should be found in every sound elementary or primary school curriculum. At the secondary level, the basic curriculum should consist of history, mathematics, science, languages, and literature. The college curriculum should consist of both the liberal arts and science. By mastering these subjects that deal with the natural and social environments, students are prepared to participate effectively in civilized society.

Although perhaps not identified as Essentialism, this theory has had a long history and definite staying power in U.S. education and schooling. When it originated in the nineteenth century, many proponents of public education believed that the goal of the common schools should be the development of a literate, skilled, and productive populace. Schooling was identified with economic productivity and growth. In the early twentieth century, social efficiency educators argued that the public school curriculum should stress those skills and subjects that contributed to economically and socially efficient lives. Periodically in U.S. educational history, concerted efforts have been made to relate education and schools to civic competency, economic skills, and social efficiency.

Clifton Fadiman has stated the case for basic education, another name for Essentialism. Basic education, he says, is concerned with subjects that have "generative power," which means the potency to endow students "with the ability to learn the higher, more complex developments of these master subjects as well as the minor or self-terminating" ones. Such generative subjects deal with "language, whether or not one's own; forms, figures, and numbers; the laws of nature; the past; and the shape and behavior of our common home, the earth."[1]

Among the common Essentialist themes are the following: (1) the elementary curriculum should emphasize basic tool skills that contribute to literacy and numeracy; (2) the secondary curriculum should include history, mathematics, science, literature, and language; (3) discipline is necessary for systematic learning in school situations; (4) respect for legitimate authority, both in school and in society, should be cultivated in students; (5) the mastering of a skill or a subject requires effort and diligence on the part of the learner; (6) the teaching of these necessary skills and subjects requires mature and well-educated teachers who know their subjects and are able to transmit them to students.

In this chapter we examine the Essentialist position, look at Arthur Bestor's curriculum of intellectual disciplines, explore basic education and the Essentialist revival, examine schooling and Essentialism, and inquire into Essentialism's philosophical and ideological relationships.

THE ESSENTIALIST POSITION

Although the basic education position has had a long history, the Essentialist doctrine was formally stated by a group of like-minded educators at the convention of the National Education Association in 1938. Reacting against what they considered the excesses of Progressive education, the Essentialists argued that the primary function of formal education was to preserve and transmit the basic elements, or essentials, of human culture.

In outlining the "Essentialist Platform," William Chandler Bagley, professor of education at Columbia University's Teachers College, stated that (1) U.S. elementary school students were failing to meet the "standards of achievement in the fundamentals of education" attained in other countries; (2) U.S. secondary school students lagged academically behind the eighteen-year-olds of other countries; (3) increasingly large numbers of high school students were essentially illiterate and could not read effectively, and because of deficiencies at the primary and intermediate levels, remedial reading programs had to be instituted in many high schools; (4) in addition to declining literacy, notable deficiencies existed in mathematics and grammar; and (5) despite increased educational expenditures in the United States, there was a noticeable increase in the rates of serious crime.

Bagley identified two specific causes of the United States' educational malaise: (1) dominant educational theories, such as Progressivism, were "essentially enfeebling," and (2) the relaxation of academic standards in many school systems had led to the policy of widespread "social promotion." Bagley chastised Progressives for overemphasizing the child's freedom, interests, and play, and for abandoning discipline, effort, and work. For Bagley, Progressive education had contributed to the "complete abandonment in many school systems of rigorous standards of scholastic achievement for promotion from grade to grade, and the passing of all pupils 'on schedule.'"[2] Instead of a curriculum based on systematic and sequential learning and consecutive, cumulative, and orderly academic development, the Progressives had substituted an undifferentiated program of activities, projects, and incidental learning. Bagley's condemnation of social promotion was similar to today's basic education arguments that students should master minimal competencies before being promoted to a higher grade or being awarded a diploma.

Bagley was joined by other professional educators such as Michael Demiashkevich, Walter H. Ryle, M. L. Shane, and Gary M. Whipple, who, calling themselves Essentialists, urged U.S. schools, teachers, and administrators to return to the basic skills of recording, computing, measuring, U.S. history, health instruction, natural science, and the fine and industrial arts. In taking their stance, the Essentialists asked:

> *Should not our public schools prepare boys and girls for adult responsibility through systematic training in such subjects as reading, writing, arithmetic, history, and English, requiring mastery of such subjects, and, when necessary, stressing discipline and obedience?*[3]

Arguing that progressive education had created discontinuity between the generations, Bagley urged U.S. educators and schools to provide each generation with "possession of a common core of ideas, meanings, understandings, and ideals representing the most precious elements of the human heritage."[4]

Although Essentialists stated their case carefully and consistently, their educational philosophy was not to prevail in the colleges of education, in teacher education, or in the professional literature. Essentialism was either neglected or relegated to a footnote in books on the history of education. Essentialism has recently reappeared in the basic education revival that argues that scholastic standards have fallen, academic rigor and sequence are absent in many schools, and that there needs to be a return to essential skills and subjects.

Bagley and his Essentialists issued a thorough rationale for the Essentialist position. Although early Essentialism has been neglected by philosophers and historians of education, the Essentialist Platform was clearly prophetic of what has proved to be a recurring critique of U.S. education and schools. Like the authors of *A Nation at Risk,* the early Essentialists used comparative and cross-cultural evidence to identify the academic deficiencies of U.S. students. They, like contemporary critics, contended that academic standards had eroded because of permissivism and progressivism. Like current critics, they attributed rising crime rates to indiscipline and a lack of standards in the schools. However, the Essentialism of the 1930s makes an interesting contrast with the contemporary movement. The early Essentialists largely came from within the ranks of professional educators; in fact, several were highly prominent professors of education. Contemporary Essentialism draws much of its support from outside of the educational profession, particularly from business leaders and from Neo-Conservative political forces.

4

BESTOR'S CURRICULUM
OF INTELLECTUAL DISCIPLINES

The basic education position surfaced again in the 1950s. Just as the earlier Essentialists had challenged Progressive education, critics in the 1950s reacted against a new educational theory called "life adjustment" that emphasized the personal and social needs of U.S. children and youth over academic subjects. Critics such as Max Rafferty, Hyman Rickover, and Arthur Bestor questioned life-adjustment education. Rafferty, who served as Superintendent of Public Instruction in California from 1963 to 1971, wrote two books, *Suffer Little Children* and *What They Are Doing to Your Children,* which attacked Progressive educators for lacking standards and for encouraging a permissiveness that had produced a generation of delinquent, unpatriotic, undereducated "slobs."[5] Admiral Hyman Rickover, who pioneered the first atomic submarine, decried the decline of U.S. academic standards in *Education and Freedom, Swiss Schools and Ours: Why Theirs are Better,* and *American Education—A National Failure.*[6] Rickover argued that U.S. public education had lowered academic standards, ignored the intellectually gifted, and neglected mathematics, science, and foreign-language instruction.

One of the most articulate critics of the 1950s, Arthur Bestor, professor of history at the University of Illinois, published *Educational Wastelands* (1953) and *The Restoration of Learning* (1956) and helped organize the Council for Basic Education.[7] According to Bestor: (1) academic standards in U.S. public schools had declined because of an anti-intellectual educational philosophy that had separated the schools from the scientific and scholarly disciplines; and (2) a narrowly educated group of professional educators, administrators, and department of education bureaucrats at the state level had gained control of entry into the teaching profession by manipulating certification requirements. Bestor urged that the trend to anti-intellectualism be reversed and that the public school curriculum be based on the intellectual disciplines of English, foreign languages, history, mathematics, and science. While the Essentialists were professional educators and the critics of the 1950s primarily were not, their arguments had much in common. Both groups believed that U.S. schools were dominated by an anti-basic education theory. For the Essentialists, it was Progressivism. For the critics of the 1950s, it was life adjustment. Both groups decried falling academic standards, declining literacy, and the absence of rigor and discipline in the schools. Bagley, Rickover, and Bestor saw European schools as having higher academic standards than U.S. schools.

In particular, Bestor's books were part of the movement to restore a basic subject-matter curriculum in the nation's schools. Some comments on his philosophy of education are useful in examining contemporary Essentialist education that emphasizes basic education and a return to intellectual disciplines as the focus of curriculum.

In *The Restoration of Learning,* Bestor established a criterion of education based on intellectual disciplines and indicated that U.S. education was failing to meet the criterion of disciplined intelligence. Strongly implied in Bestor's educational theory is a conception of U.S. democracy based on the rule of reasonable and intelligent citizens. An intelligently functioning democracy is a government of law, orderly parliamentary processes, and democratic guarantees for all citizens. Bestor expressed a definite Essentialist theory of education which provides

> *sound training in the fundamental ways of thinking represented by history, science, mathematics, literature, language, art and other disciplines evolved in the course of mankind's long quest for usable knowledge, cultural understanding, and intellectual power.*[8]

These intellectual disciplines should be fundamental in the school curriculum for they are basic in modern life. In the elementary school, reading, writing, and arithmetic provide indispensable generative skills. The essentials of the secondary school curriculum are science, mathematics, history, English, and foreign languages. These intellectual disciplines, the core of a liberal education, are humankind's most reliable tools in solving personal, social, political, and economic problems.

Bestor sought to achieve his educational ideal through an essential subject-matter curriculum based on history, mathematics, science, foreign languages, and English. Indeed, the years devoted to the pursuit of formal learning are based on these five essential intellectual disciplines. During the first four, five, or six years of schooling, reading, writing, and arithmetic are the necessary generative tool skills. The elementary school student should also be introduced to the structures and methods of the natural sciences, geography, and history.[9]

Junior high school, the grades from seven to nine, marks the beginning of organized and systematic study. A transition is made from arithmetic to the more abstract forms of mathematical reasoning, beginning with elementary algebra. History is to assume a recognized chronological structure. From the generalized natural science studied earlier, a transition is made as the student is introduced to sciences such as biology, physics, or chemistry. Instruction in foreign languages moves forward to grammatical analysis.

Students in the senior high school are expected to pursue a subject methodologically and to use abstract reasoning. Specifically, the study of mathematics is continued through advanced algebra, plane geometry, trigonometry, analytical geometry, and calculus. Systematic work in chemistry, physics, and biology furnishes the needed foundations of scientific knowledge. History's chronological pattern and structure are emphasized. English is employed with accuracy, lucidity, and grace. One foreign language is mastered and another begun.[10]

Bestor's proposed curriculum is prescribed for all students. Once he or she has mastered these essentials, the student can begin vocational or college education. Training in the liberating disciplines prepares a person for intellectual life, citizenship, a vocation, and for a profession.

Bestor feared that U.S. schools were failing to provide the needed intellectual discipline. He charged that some professional educators postulated an erroneous view of a democratic education. Because the intellectual disciplines were once reserved to aristocratic elites, these educators failed to realize that the progress of the modern age now made an intellectual education the prerogative of all.

Bestor charged that professional educators, no longer content with methodology, had usurped curriculum making. Curriculum construction is best exercised by the scholars and scientists who are expert in their academic disciplines. Some professional educators had distorted Progressive education into a "regressive education," according to Bestor. They had watered down the great intellectual disciplines and introduced vocational and life-adjustment courses into the general curriculum to the detriment of the academic subjects. By weakening liberal education, too much of public education had become anti-democratic and anti-intellectual.

Bestor's educational agenda emphasized two fundamental principles: (1) ensuring disciplined intellectual education to every future citizen, and (2) providing opportunity for advanced study to all who possess genuine intellectual capacity and a willingness to develop their intellectual powers.[11]

These two principles serve as the basis of the school's primary responsibilities, which are outlined as follows: (1) the school should provide a standard program of intellectual training in the fundamental disciplines geared to the needs of serious students and to the capacities of the upper two-thirds of the school population; (2) the school should provide special opportunities for exceptionally able students; (3) programs designed for the highest third of the school population should be balanced with adequate remedial programs for the lowest third, the slow learners; (4) a program of physical education for all children should be provided that is distinguished from interschool athletics; (5) the school should diversify its offerings to include certain areas of vocational training; (6) there should be certain extracurricular activities; (7) high-ability students should continue in school; (8) life-adjustment training should be provided only for the least able and least ambitious.[12]

Bestor's proposed reform runs counter to the Progressive views of education. The chief contention is evident in this quotation from Bestor's *The Restoration of Learning:* "The school makes itself ridiculous whenever it undertakes to deal directly with 'real-life' problems, instead of indirectly through the development of generalized intellectual powers."[13]

BASIC EDUCATION AND THE ESSENTIALIST REVIVAL

A recent revival of Essentialism in the United States is the movement for "basic" education. In some respects, this movement, like the earlier Essentialist one, generated from criticisms of U.S. public schools. Basic-education proponents used comparisons with education in other countries, often Germany and Japan, for evidence that U.S. academic standards and achievement had declined. Among the criticisms that proponents of basic education have levied are the following:

1. Permissive, open, and progressive educational methods have neglected basic skills of reading, writing, and arithmetic, and have contributed to a growing functional illiteracy.
2. Schools do not stress fundamental values of industriousness, punctuality, effort, morality, or patriotism.
3. Teachers are ill prepared and undereducated; those teachers who strive for academic excellence find themselves thwarted by inefficient, expensive, and mindless educational bureaucracies.
4. Recent curricular innovations have neglected fundamental skills and subjects. Further, the confusing jargon of the "new math, new social studies, and new science" has made it difficult for parents to be involved in and to monitor their children's education.
5. Social-promotion policies rather than academic achievement have dumped ill-prepared and undereducated high school graduates on the society and the economy.
6. Schools have been used for social engineering and experimentation rather than for basic education. Administrators and teachers perform so many noneducational functions that they neglect the basics.
7. Educational expenses could be contained by reducing nonacademic frills, eliminating electives, and concentrating on required basic skills and subjects.
8. Permissive policies have contributed to violence and vandalism in the schools.
9. Minority groups such as African Americans and Hispanics have been shortchanged by the schools with respect to instruction in the basic skills.
10. U.S. industrial and business productivity has been reduced by undereducated graduates who cannot perform fundamental skills, who cannot read or write effectively, and who lack productive work skills and habits.

The revival of basic education took three lines of development. One, the Council for Basic Education continued to emphasize intellectual content from a liberal arts and sciences perspective. The Council for Basic Education emphasized intellectual content from a liberal arts and sciences perspective. The second line of development emerged from a coalition of some parents, businesspersons, politicians, and occasionally professional educators, who were dissatisfied with public education for a variety of reasons, among them, declining test scores, a decline of traditional patriotic and moral values, increasing drug abuse, and the weakening of the economic position of the United States relative to foreign competitors. Although these critics had varying motives, they were united in demanding a return to basic skills, subjects, and values.[14] The third line of development came under the auspices of the federal government, under the leadership of Terrel Bell, Secretary of Education in the Reagan administration, with the publication in 1983 of *A Nation at Risk.*

Like other reports calling for a return to rigorous academic standards, *A Nation at Risk* warned that "the educational foundations of our society are presently being eroded by a rising tide of mediocrity that threatens our very future as a Nation and a people."[15] Echoing the criticisms of Bagley and Bestor, the National Commission on Excellence reported its findings. Among them were the following:

Secondary school curricula have been homogenized, diluted and diffused to the point that they no longer have a central purpose.[16]

In many other industrialized nations, courses in mathematics (other than arithmetic or general mathematics), biology, chemistry, physics, and geography start in grade 6 and are required of all students. The time spent on these subjects, based on class hours, is about three times that spent by even the most science-oriented U.S. students, i.e., those who select 4 years of science and mathematics in secondary school.[17]

In many schools, the time spent learning how to cook and drive counts as much toward a high school diploma as the time spent studying mathematics, English, chemistry, U.S. history, or biology.[18]

Leaning heavily in the direction of a content-oriented and subject-matter curriculum, the Commission on Excellence recommended

that State and local high school graduation requirements be strengthened and that, at a minimum, all students seeking a diploma be required to lay the foundations in the Five New Basics by taking the following curriculum during their 4 years of high school: (a) 4 years of English; (b) 3 years of mathematics; (c) 3 years of science; (d) 3 years of social studies; and (e) one-half year of computer science. For the college-bound, 2 years of foreign language in high school are strongly recommended in addition to those taken earlier.[19]

and

that schools, colleges, and universities adopt more rigorous and measurable standards, and higher expectations, for academic performance and student conduct, and that 4-year colleges and universities raise their requirements for admission. This will help students do their best educationally with challenging materials in an environment that supports learning and authentic accomplishment.[20]

A Nation at Risk stimulated other national reports and educational recommendations that urged emphasis on basic skills and subjects. For example, the Task Force on Education for Economic Growth, in *Action for Excellence*, stressed basic skills and competencies for productive employment in a structurally and technologically changing society.[21] The College Board in *Academic Preparation for College* identified the basic academic competencies or "broad intellectual skills essential to effective work" in college as reading, speaking and listening, writing, mathematics, reasoning, and studying. Added to this conventional list of tool skills was a basic knowledge of computer processes, terminology, and application.[22] The College Board identified the basic academic subjects that provide "the detailed knowledge and skills" for effective college work as English, the arts, mathematics, science, social studies, and foreign languages.[23]

Essentialism also has reappeared in the arguments of commentators such as E. D. Hirsch, Jr., Chester Finn, and Diane Ravitch who contend that public schools are failing to impart the knowledge needed for cultural and political literacy. For example, E. D. Hirsch, Jr., argues that the average American's declining cultural literacy, the lack of a shared body of common knowledge, is negatively impacting a sense of a national cultural identity and ability to communicate effectively with other Americans. Because the contemporary school curriculum does not deliberately transmit a core to develop cultural literacy, many students complete their formal education without the necessary contextual background that enables them to reference and interpret materials crucial for public communication and for effective functioning in the workplace. A core curriculum designed to promote cultural literacy, Hirsch contends, is needed if citizens are to participate in the institutions and processes of political democracy.[24]

SCHOOLING AND ESSENTIALISM

Essentialism defines the role of schooling in strictly academic terms. For Essentialists, the term *academic,* too, is specifically defined as foundational skills and intellectual subject matters. Essentialists do not like vaguely constructed or broadly defined educational agendas that move the educational process into non-academic areas. This tendency, found among Progressives and Social Reconstructionists, for example, confuses the purpose of the schools, according to Essentialists.

Just as the school's function is specifically defined, the curriculum, too, is specific in terms of generative tool skills and academic subjects. Further, the curriculum is considered too important by Essentialists to be determined by shifting social fads and tendencies and by childish whims. Essentialists argue that educators must carefully structure the curriculum according to scope and sequence. Each grade level should have a particular set of objectives to guide instruction. Each teacher must have a particular set of skills or a well-defined academic subject to teach. It is important that the schools be administered so that each skill or subject is taught in an articulated manner, with one phase of instruction leading to the next. Further, instruction should be cumulative in that each phase builds on the preceding phase and leads to the next.

Essentialists argue that although schools are part of a societal context, they are effective when they fulfill their primary academic function. Knowledge of the social context should help teachers do their academic jobs more effectively and efficiently. It should also help administrators and teachers perform their primary tasks more effectively and efficiently. However, the existence of social problems should not deter teachers from performing their academic tasks, nor should these social issues be allowed to alter the primary function of schools. The Essentialist view is that large social problems are at base political, economic, and social issues that need to be addressed by agencies outside of the school, whose functions are appropriate in dealing with these problems. Although educators need to understand social problems and how they impact education, teachers do not have it in their power to cure society's ills. They do have it in their power, however, to teach reading, writing, history, and science, for example. By providing academic literacy, schools can build a civic knowledge base in an informed citizenry that can then use their informed intelligence to resolve social issues.

For the Essentialist, the examination of social, political, and economic issues are part of the exploration of the academic knowledge base. Here the academic subject either reaches its current or applied state. For example, poverty, drug abuse, and racism might be part of an academic exploration of subject matter. The objective is to understand trends and tendencies in a particular academic subject. The function of the school is to examine issues academically, not to solve them in the school. Indeed, the Essentialist is likely to argue that it is beyond the school's power to solve social problems. The school does its job when it educates an intelligent citizenry and a competent work force by imparting the necessary skills and knowledge of subject matter.

ESSENTIALISM'S PHILOSOPHICAL AND IDEOLOGICAL RELATIONSHIPS

As an educational theory, Essentialism exhibits certain themes that are parallel with the more traditional philosophies of Idealism, Realism, and Thomism discussed earlier. (To review these themes, you may wish to refer to Chapters 2, 3, and 4.) Like these philosophies, Essentialism's educational perspective stresses the transmission to the young of a structured and orderly view of reality. While the Idealist, Realist, and Thomist conceptions of reality are metaphysical, the Essentialist preference for order and structure is primarily social, economic, and cultural. It should be pointed out, however, that some Essentialists derived their position from one of these traditional philosophies.

In terms of an ideological orientation, Essentialism parallels most closely the Conservative view that sees education's primary function as that of transmitting the funded and approved knowledge and values of the culture. It also bears some resemblance to the Liberal perspective, particularly the Classical Liberal variety, which emphasizes the skills, knowledge, and values that enhance social and economic efficiency. Essentialism is highly compatible with those aspects of the contemporary Neo-Conservative ideology that emphasizes a need to (1) enhance U.S. economic productivity in a highly competitive global economy;

(2) restore standards of civility and academic achievement in public schools; (3) structure the curriculum around the fundamental skills and subjects that contribute to social, economic, and political efficiency; and (4) oppose those educators who would weaken the schools' primary academic mission.

The Essentialist position opposes certain aspects of Naturalism, Pragmatism, and Existentialism, which were discussed in Chapters 5, 6, and 7. Unlike the Naturalists, who stress the educational potency of the person's feelings and emotions, Essentialists emphasize the primary importance of the human mind as an instrument best cultivated by intellectual disciplines. While Pragmatists stress an open and evolutionary universe of constant change, Essentialists want education, especially schooling, to provide human beings with a secure and stable reference point. Whereas Existentialists stress human subjectivity and self-definition, Essentialists are more concerned with transmitting an antecedent curriculum to learners.

For the Essentialist, the school has the specific function of transmitting to the young certain generative skills and certain general intellectual disciplines. By transmitting these skills and subjects, the school perpetuates the cultural heritage. Conservatives would concur with Essentialists that the school is to be an agency of cultural continuity and stability. Essentialists would argue that the more the society shows symptoms of social malaise, the more important it is for schools to be stable academic environments for students.

The term *essential* means that the school, in performing its role as a cultural transmitter, identifies and perpetuates the basic cultural elements. It is not to take on nonessential functions such as "social adjustment," career education, consumer education, cooking classes, and other such activities that should be learned elsewhere. For the school to assume responsibility for these nonessentials would mean that the essential core of necessary skills and subjects would be diluted or diminished.

For Essentialists and the contemporary proponents of basic education, the school's primary mission is academic. It is not an agency to promote social engineering, as Utopians or Social Reconstructionists assert. Sharing the Conservative's suspicion of innovation and change, Essentialists would oppose using the schools as experimental laboratories to test curricular or instructional innovations. Untested innovation creates an unsettled atmosphere that weakens the school's essential or basic function.

Primarily an educational theory that focuses on schooling rather than on large socioeconomic issues, Essentialism has a well-defined curricular orientation. Essentialists assert that the curriculum should provide students with a differentiated and organized learning experience rather than an undifferentiated experience that students must organize themselves. The most effective and efficient mode of providing a differentiated educational experience is the subject-matter curriculum in which each subject or intellectual discipline is organized separately from other subjects. Further, each subject is organized according to carefully arranged principles of scope and sequence.

The Essentialists reject curricular innovations, such as Experimentalist problem solving or Progressive projects, which seek to break down subject-matter boundaries. Such undifferentiated curricular designs, contend the Essentialists, are inefficient in that they often force students to "reinvent the wheel" rather than learning and using the fund of knowledge that already exists. Moreover, these undifferentiated educational approaches are presumptuous in that they assume that students can take some elements from a subject without knowing the context from which it comes. Essentialists would condemn the Pragmatist, Reconstructionist, and Progressive approaches to learning as contributing to an academic confusion that weakens intellectual authority and social organization.

Essentialists, like the adherents to traditional philosophies and Conservative ideology, assert that the teacher is an academic authority figure. The teacher is to be a specialist in the content of the subject matter and be skilled in organizing it for instructional purposes. While the Essentialist teacher speaks with the sense of authority that knowledge brings, this should not be confused with authoritarianism. Defenders of intellectual disciplines, such as Arthur Bestor, argue that the liberal knowledge that they contain and convey is the best guarantee for preserving both academic freedom in the school and civil liberties in society.

CONCLUSION

Essentialism is the educational theory that sees the primary function of the school as the preservation and transmission of the basic elements of human culture. It emphasizes (1) a return to systematic subjects, (2) learning as the mastery of basic skills and knowledge, (3) the teacher as a mature representative of the culture and someone who is competent in both subject matter and instruction, (4) education as preparation for work and citizenship, and (5) the preservation of the school's academic function. Above all, Essentialists oppose catering to childish whims or to transitory fads that will cause schools to degenerate into mindless and irrelevant institutions.

DISCUSSION QUESTIONS

1. Define Essentialism and indicate how the term applies to the school and the curriculum.

2. Examine the Essentialist critique. Does it resemble contemporary criticisms of U.S. public schooling?

3. Examine Arthur Bestor's rationale for a curriculum based on intellectual disciplines. Compare and contrast Bestor's proposed curriculum with that recommended in *A Nation at Risk*.

4. Why has there been a resurgence of the basic-education theory in the United States?

5. Reflect on your own educational experience. To what extent does it resemble or differ from an Essentialist or basic-education perspective?

6. Of the philosophies examined in this text, which is most compatible and which is least compatible with Essentialism or basic education?

7. Of the ideologies examined in this text, which is the most compatible and which is the least compatible with the Essentialist or basic-education theory?

INQUIRY PROJECTS

- Identify the key points in the Essentialist critique. In a paper, examine contemporary criticisms of public schooling found in reports such as *A Nation at Risk* and *Action for Excellence*. Do these criticisms parallel those made by the Essentialists?
- Examine and review selected publications of the Council for Basic Education.
- Review a book on education written by one of the following: Arthur Bestor, Max Rafferty, Clifton Fadiman, James Koerner, Hyman Rickover, or Diane Ravitch.
- Collect "letters to the editor" or other public-opinion pieces on education. Determine if these items reflect a basic-education perspective.
- Consult curriculum or methods books used in courses in teacher education at your college or university. To what degree do they reflect or disagree with the Essentialist or basic-education theory?
- Visit several schools and observe the curricular organization and instructional methods being used. To what extent do they reflect or disagree with the Essentialist or basic-education theory?

FURTHER READINGS

Bestor, Arthur E., Jr. *Educational Wastelands: Retreat from Learning in Our Public Schools.* Urbana: University of Illinois Press, 1953.

Bestor, Arthur E., Jr. *The Restoration of Learning: A Program for Redeeming the Unfulfilled Promise of American Education.* New York: Alfred A. Knopf, 1956.

Brodinsky, Ben. *Defining the Basics of American Education.* Bloomington, IN: Phi Delta Kappa Educational Foundation, 1977.

Bunzel, John H., ed. *Challenge to American Schools: The Case for Standards and Values.* New York: Oxford University Press, 1985.

French, Peter A., Theodore E. Uehling, and Howard K. Wettstein, eds. *Studies in Essentialism.* Minneapolis: University of Minnesota Press, 1986.

Gutek, Gerald L. *Basic Education: A Historical Perspective.* Bloomington, IN: Phi Delta Kappa Educational Foundation, 1981.

Hirsch, E. D., Jr. *Cultural Literacy: What Every American Needs to Know.* Boston: Houghton Mifflin, 1987.

Kandel, Isaac L. *William Chandler Bagley: Stalwart Educator.* New York: Teachers College Press, 1961.

Koerner, James D., ed. *The Case for Basic Education.* Boston: Little, Brown, 1959.

National Commission on Excellence in Education. *A Nation at Risk: The Imperative for Educational Reform.* Washington, DC: U.S. Department of Education, 1983.

The Nation Responds: Recent Efforts to Improve Education. Washington, DC: U.S. Department of Education, 1984.

Pursell, William. *A Conservative Alternative School: The A+ School in Cupertino.* Bloomington, IN: Phi Delta Kappa Educational Foundation, 1976.

Rafferty, Max. *Suffer Little Children.* New York: Signet, 1962.

Rafferty, Max. *What They Are Doing to Your Children.* New York: New American Library, 1963.

Rickover, H. G. *American Education—A National Failure.* New York: E. P. Dutton, 1963.

Rickover, H. G. *Education and Freedom.* New York: E. P. Dutton, 1959.

Rickover, H. G. *Swiss Schools and Ours: Why Theirs Are Better.* Boston: Atlantic–Little, Brown, 1962.

Sewall, Gilbert T. *Necessary Lessons: Decline and Renewal in American Schools.* New York: The Free Press, 1983.

Sommer, Carl. *Schools in Crisis: Training for Success or Failure?* Houston, TX: Cahill, 1984.

Task Force on Education for Economic Growth. *Action for Excellence.* Denver, CO: Education Commission of the States, 1983.

The College Board. *Academic Preparation for College: What Students Need to Know and Be Able to Do.* New York: The College Board, 1983.

ENDNOTES

1. Clifton Fadiman, "The Case for Basic Education," in James D. Koerner, ed., *The Case for Basic Education* (Boston: Little, Brown, 1959), pp. 5–6.

2. William C. Bagley, "An Essentialist's Platform for the Advancement of American Education," *Educational Administration and Supervision,* XXIV (April 1938): 241–256.

3. Adolphe E. Meyer, *The Development of Education in the Twentieth Century* (Englewood Cliffs, NJ: Prentice Hall, 1949), p. 149.

4. Bagley, "An Essentialist's Platform," p. 254.

5. Max Rafferty, *Suffer Little Children* (New York: Signet, 1962); *What They Are Doing to Your Children* (New York: New American Library, 1963).

6. H. G. Rickover, *Swiss Schools and Ours: Why Theirs Are Better* (Boston: Atlantic–Little, Brown, 1962); *Education and Freedom* (New York: E. P. Dutton,

1959); *American Education—A National Failure* (New York: E. P. Dutton, 1963).

7. Arthur Bestor, *Educational Wastelands: Retreat from Learning in Our Public Schools* (Urbana: University of Illinois Press, 1953); *The Restoration of Learning: A Program for Redeeming the Unfulfilled Promise of American Education* (New York: Alfred A. Knopf, 1956).

8. Bestor, *The Restoration of Learning,* p. 7.

9. Ibid., pp. 50–51.

10. Ibid.

11. Ibid., p. 358.

12. Ibid., pp. 364–365.

13. Ibid., p. 79.

14. Gerald L. Gutek, *Basic Education: A Historical Perspective* (Bloomington, IN: Phi Delta Kappa Educational Foundation, 1981), pp. 9–13.

15. National Commission on Excellence in Education, *A Nation at Risk: The Imperative for Educational Reform* (Wash-

ington, DC: U.S. Department of Education, 1983), p. 5.

16. Ibid., p. 18.

17. Ibid., p. 20.

18. Ibid., p. 22.

19. Ibid., p. 24.

20. Ibid., p. 27.

21. Task Force on Education for Economic Growth, *Action for Excellence* (Denver, CO: Education Commission of the States, 1983), p. 48.

22. The College Board, *Academic Preparation for College: What Students Need to Know and Be Able to Do* (New York: The College Board, 1983), pp. 7–11.

23. Ibid., p. 13.

24. E. D. Hirsch, Jr., *Cultural Literacy: What Every American Needs to Know* (Boston: Houghton Mifflin, 1987).

Chapter 2

Perennialism and Education

The Perennialist theory of education draws heavily from the Realist and Thomist philosophies, examined earlier in this book. Metaphysically, the Perennialists proclaim the intellectual and spiritual character of the universe and the human place within it. Following the Aristotelian premise that human beings are rational creatures, the Perennialists see the school as a social institution specifically designed to develop human intellectual potentiality. The term *Perennialism* comes from the assertion that the important principles of education are changeless and recurrent. For the Perennialist, the educational philosopher's first problem is to examine human nature and to devise an educational program based on its universal characteristics. Among these characteristics are the following: (1) Our human intellect enables us to frame alternative propositions and to choose those that fulfill the requirements of our human nature. Because we can frame and choose between alternatives, we are free agents. (2) The basic human values derive from our rationality, which defines us as human. People everywhere frame their thoughts in symbolic patterns and communicate them to others. (3) Although cultural particularities exist, humans everywhere have framed ethical principles that govern their individual and corporate lives. Throughout the world, people of varying languages and cultures have developed religious and aesthetic modes of experience and expression.

Because human nature is constant, Perennialists assert, so are the basic patterns of education. Foremost, education should aim to cultivate rational powers. Basically, the universal aim of education is truth. And because that which is true is universal and unchanging, a genuine education should also be universal and constant. The school's curriculum should emphasize the universal and recurrent themes of human life. It should contain cognitive materials designed to cultivate rationality; it should be highly logical and enable students to use the symbolic patterns of thought and communication. It should cultivate ethical principles and encourage moral, aesthetic, and religious criticism and appreciation. The Perennialist educational theory seeks to develop the intellectual and spiritual potentialities of the child to their fullest extent through a subject-matter curriculum based on such disciplines as history, language, mathematics, logic, literature, the humanities, and science. These subjects, regarded as bearing the knowledge of the human race, are the tools of civilized people and have a disciplinary effect on the human mind.

Perennialist educational theory emphasizes the humanities as providing insights into the good, true, and beautiful. In these works, humankind has captured a glimpse of the eternal truths and values. Such insights, found in science, philosophy, literature, history, and art, persist as they are transmitted from generation to generation. Works such as those of Plato, Aristotle, and John Stuart Mill, for example, possess a quality that makes them perennially appealing to people living at different times and in different places. Other ideas, which may be popular to a particular time but fail to meet the test of time, are discarded.

These general principles associated with Perennialism can be seen by examining the educational ideas of Robert M. Hutchins and Jacques Maritain. While Hutchins represents a more secular variety of classical humanism, Maritain has been identified with the religious Perennialism associated with Neo-Thomistic philosophy. Although certain important variations exist in the philosophical positions of both Hutchins and Maritain, there is agreement on the following basic principles: (1) a body of truth exists that is universally valid regardless of circumstances and contingencies; (2) a sound education will contribute to the pursuit of truth and to the cultivation of the permanent principles of right and justice; and (3) truth can be taught best through the systematic study and analysis of the human past—as portrayed in the great works of religion, philosophy, literature, and history. In addition to examining the ideas of Hutchins and Maritain, we will also discuss the Paideia proposal as a revival of Perennialism. We will then examine Perennialism in relationship to the other philosophies and ideologies treated in this text.

ROBERT M. HUTCHINS

Robert Maynard Hutchins (1899–1977) was an articulate advocate of the proposition that education is properly devoted to the cultivation of the human intellect. Hutchins received his higher education at Yale University. From 1927 to 1929 he was a professor of law at Yale. At age thirty, he became president of the University of Chicago and served until he became chancellor of that university in 1945.[1] In 1954, Hutchins was named head of the Fund for the Republic. He was associated with the Center for the Study of Democratic Institutions, a nonprofit educational enterprise established by the Fund for the Republic to promote the principles of individual liberty in a democratic society. Hutchins spoke and wrote on liberal education. His major educational works include *The Higher Learning in America* (1936), *Education for Freedom* (1943), *Conflict in Education in a Democratic Society* (1953), *University of Utopia* (1953), and *The Learning Society* (1968).[2]

When asked his opinion as to the ideal education, Hutchins replied:

Ideal education is the one that develops intellectual power. I arrive at this conclusion by a process of elimination. Educational institutions are the only institutions that can develop intellectual power. The ideal education is not an ad hoc education, not an education directed to immediate needs; it is not a specialized education, or a pre-professional education; it is not a utilitarian education. It is an education calculated to develop the mind.

There may be many ways, all equally good, of developing the mind. I have old-fashioned prejudices in favor of the three R's and the liberal arts, in favor of trying to understand the greatest works that the human race has produced. I believe that these are the permanent necessities, the intellectual tools that are needed to understand the ideas and ideals of our world. This does not exclude later specialization or later professional education; but I insist that without the intellectual techniques needed to understand ideas, and without at least an acquaintance with the major ideas that have animated mankind since the dawn of history, no man may call himself educated.[3]

Hutchins's words reveal some basic principles of his educational philosophy. He believed that: (1) a cultivation of the foundational skills of reading, writing, and arithmetic was indispensable for literate and civilized people; (2) a liberal education should contribute to an understanding of the great works of civilization; and (3) professional and specialized education should be deferred until one has completed general education, an education every person should have as a rational human being.

In 1936, Hutchins published *The Higher Learning in America*, which was a critique of both higher education and general education. Commentary on this work is useful in establishing Hutchins's educational perspective.

Hutchins based his educational philosophy on two basic concepts: (1) humans' rational nature; and (2) a conception of knowledge based on eternal, absolute, and universal truths. His educational theory assumes the presence in human nature of essential and unchanging elements. Believing that human nature was everywhere the same, Hutchins stressed a universal education. Because rationality is the highest attribute of human nature, the cultivation of the intellect is education's highest goal.[4] The intellectual virtues lead to the discovery of the great truths found in the classic works of Western civilization.

Unfortunately, U.S. education has failed to devote its energies to the pursuit of truth and to the cultivation of intellectual excellence. U.S. higher education, in particular, has become misdirected because of confusion that exists in the society external to education. Three factors, Hutchins asserted, have contributed to this general confusion: (1) love of money, (2) an erroneous conception of democracy, and (3) a false notion of progress. Immersed in materialism and catering to the shifting whims of students, donors, business interests, alumni, and politicians, Hutchins claimed that the university had lost its integrity in the frantic search for operating funds. Contemporary America had witnessed the rise of a university that was much like a service station. In contrast, Hutchins argued for a university whose sole purpose was to pursue and discover truth.

Hutchins believed that a confused conception of democracy had resulted in the commonly held belief that everyone should receive the same amount and degree of education. He would reserve higher education for students who have the interest and ability for independent intellectual activity. A false notion of progress had led to the rejection of the wisdom of the past, which had been replaced by a belief that progress comes only from empiricism and materialism. A superficial empiricism had confused knowledge with the mere collection of information and data, according to Hutchins. This confusion had produced an anti-intellectualism that regarded the most worthwhile education as that bringing the greatest financial return.

U.S. higher education was not only beset by confusion from external sources, but it also had its own internal conditions of disintegration, such as professionalism, isolation, and anti-intellectualism. Professionalism, resulting from the surrender of the university to vocational pressures, was motivated by the perverted utilitarianism that equated making money with knowledge. Hutchins's attack on premature professionalism was based on three main arguments: (1) school instruction lags behind actual practice; (2) it is foolish to try to master constantly changing techniques; and (3) direct experience is the most efficient source of practical wisdom.

Overspecialization has isolated specialist from specialist, Hutchins said. Without the integrating core of a common education, specialists lacked the ideas and language that came from shared and communicable experience. Anti-intellectualism stems from an emphasis on the purely utilitarian at the cost of sacrificing theory and speculation. Hutchins asserted that theoretical knowledge was essential to human rationality.

Hutchins claimed that vocationalism and specialized education had entered the curriculum prematurely and had distorted the purposes of general education. An overemphasis on specialization had pushed the liberal arts out of the general curriculum. Some educators had tied education to specific political and social programs that led to either superficiality or indoctrination rather than to critical intelligence.

The Curriculum: The Permanent Studies

Hutchins argued that the curriculum should be composed of permanent studies that reflect the common elements of human nature and connect each generation to the best thoughts of humankind. He particularly recommended the study of the "great books"—classics contemporary in any age. The great books of the Western world embraced all areas of knowledge, according to Hutchins. He believed that four years spent reading and discussing the great books would cultivate standards of judgment and criticism and prepare students to think carefully and act intelligently.

In addition to the great books of Western civilization, Hutchins recommended the study of grammar, rhetoric, logic, and mathematics. Grammar, the analysis of language, contributed to the understanding and comprehension of the written word. Rhetoric provided the student with the rules of writing and speaking needed for intelligent expression; logic, the critical study of reasoning, enabled a person to think and express him- or herself in an orderly and systematic fashion. Mathematics was of general value as it represented reasoning in its clearest and most precise form.

In order to restore rationality in higher education, Hutchins advocated the revitalizing of metaphysics. As the study of first principles, he believed metaphysics pervaded the entire range of intellectual pursuits. Proceeding from the study of first principles to the most current concerns, higher education should examine fundamental human problems. Whereas the social sciences embrace the practical sciences of ethics, politics, and economics, the natural sciences deal with the study of natural and physical phenomena.

Hutchins, who was critical of the specialization that had occurred in teacher education, believed that prospective teachers should have a good general education in the liberal arts and sciences. Such an education contained the basic rules of pedagogy. The liberal arts—grammar, rhetoric, logic, and mathematics—were potent instruments in preparing the prospective teacher to organize, express, and communicate knowledge.

RELIGIOUS PERENNIALISM

The ecclesiastical varieties of Perennialism are found in the educational philosophies of the Neo-Thomists, who are often associated with Roman Catholic education.[5] Like their more secular conferees, the ecclesiastical Perennialists also believe in universal truths and values. These religious Perennialists believe in a permanent or perennial curriculum useful for all people regardless of the contingencies of differing cultures. The religious Perennialists stress that the universe and human beings within it were created by a supreme being who is a knowing and loving God. They see divine purpose operating within the laws of the universe and within human life. The religious variety of Perennialism finds expression in the philosophy of Jacques Maritain, who has also been classified as a Neo-Thomist or Integral Realist.

Jacques Maritain

Jacques Maritain was born in France in 1882 and was educated at the University of Paris. He was born into a Protestant family but became a convert to Roman Catholicism in 1906. Dissatisfied with the skepticism among academic philosophers, Maritain was attracted to the philosophy of Henri Bergson. He later came to urge a reconciliation of faith and reason in philosophy, as exemplified in the works of Thomas Aquinas. Maritain was an astute proponent of Neo-Thomist integral realism and wrote extensively on that subject. His books include such works as *Education at the Crossroads* (1943), *Man and the State* (1951), *On the Use of Philosophy* (1961), and *Integral Humanism* (1968).

Maritain's theory of education is expressed in *Education at the Crossroads,* in which he argued that the purposes of education were twofold: to educate persons to cultivate their humanity and to introduce them to their cultural heritage. Emphasis is given to the cultivation of rationality and spirituality, which define human character. Vocational and professional training he considered subordinate to the cultivation of the intellect.

Like Hutchins, Maritain condemned certain misconceptions that distorted education's true purposes. Influenced by Pragmatism, he believed that modern education, by overemphasizing means, had failed to distinguish between means and ends. The obsession with means had produced an aimless education devoid of guiding principles. Maritain asserted that the proper end of education was to educate people to realize their human potentialities. Genuine education rested on a conception of human nature based on the Judeo-Christian heritage. According to Maritain, education should guide individuals to shape themselves as human persons "armed with knowledge, strength of judgment, and moral virtues" while transmitting the "spiritual heritage" of their "nation and the civilization." Thus, it preserves "the century-old achievements of generations." While the vocational aspect of education is not to be disregarded, it "must never imperil the essential aim of education."[6]

Maritain attacked the "voluntarism" of Naturalists such as Rousseau and the Progressives who exaggerated the human being's emotional and volitional character. In seeking to educate the good-hearted person, the Naturalists neglected or minimized the cultivation of intelligent judgment. In contrast, Maritain argued that a simplistic emotionalism was inadequate. Indeed, he saw the properly functioning person as governed by intellect rather than emotionalism. Even more dangerous than Rousseauean voluntarism, according to Maritain, was the modern emphasis that urged the complete liberation of the emotions and that would make education a matter of feeling rather than thinking.

Maritain viewed the teacher as an educated, cultivated, and mature person who possessed knowledge that the students did not have but wished to acquire.

Good teaching should begin with what students already know and lead them to what they do not know. Maritain saw the teacher as a dynamic agent in the learning process.

The student, a rational and free being possessed of a spiritual soul and a corporeal body, was endowed with an intellect that sought to know. The good teacher should establish an orderly but open climate of learning that avoids the excesses of both anarchy and despotism, for the anarchical classroom rejects any kind of discipline and, with a misguided permissiveness, caters to childish whims. The despotic classroom, through fear of corporal or psychological punishment, reduces students' individuality to a standardized conformity in which spontaneity and creativity are punished as undesirable deviations.

The teacher's task is to foster those fundamental dispositions that enable students to realize their human potentialities. According to Maritain, the basic dispositions to be fostered by education are (1) love of truth, (2) love of goodness and justice, (3) simplicity and openness with regard to existence, (4) a sense of a job well done, and (5) a sense of cooperation. These five basic dispositions are to be cultivated by teachers capable of fostering growth of students' mental lives.

Maritain's Curriculum

Maritain recommended a subject-matter curriculum based on the systematic learned disciplines. Primary education, he contended, was to cultivate the basic skills needed for the successful study of the more systematic disciplines. Maritain argued against the view that the child is a miniature adult. The child's world, instead, was one of imagination. Primary teachers should begin their instruction within the child's own world of imagination and, through the use of stories and storylike narrations, lead the child to explore the objects and values of the rational world. Although the child's initial stimulus is through imagination, he or she gradually comes to exercise intellect in grasping the realities of the external world.

Maritain believed that both secondary education and higher education should be devoted to the cultivation of judgment and intellectuality through the study of the humanities. Secondary education, in particular, was to introduce the adolescent to the world of thought and to the great achievements of the human mind. Among the subjects that Maritain recommended for study in the secondary schools were grammar, foreign languages, history, geography, and the natural sciences.

Maritain divided the college curriculum into four years of study: (1) a year of mathematics and poetry when students study both these subjects and literature, logic, foreign languages, and the history of civilization; (2) a year of natural science and fine arts, which is devoted to physics, natural sciences, fine arts, mathematics, literature, poetry, and the history of science; (3) a year of philosophy, which includes the study of metaphysics, philosophy of nature, epistemology, psychology, physics and natural science, mathematics, literature, poetry, and fine arts; and (4) the last year—the year of ethical and political philosophy, which includes the examination of ethics, political and social philosophy, physics, natural science, mathematics, literature, poetry, fine arts, the history of civilization, and the history of science.

The Relationship between Theology and Philosophy

Maritain was concerned that modern society, with its stress on specialization, had destroyed the sense of integration that gives order and purpose to life. Hutchins, who shared a similar concern, recommended the revitalization of metaphysics to integrate the natural and social sciences. In recommending an education that contributed to the integration of human knowledge, Maritain contended that philosophy, which deals with human relationships to the universe, and theology, which deals with relationships to God, should be at the summit of the hierarchy of learned disciplines. As the most general and integrating of the disciplines, theology and philosophy were to provide the unity that would overcome specialization's disintegrating tendencies.

THE PAIDEIA PROPOSAL: A REVIVAL OF PERENNIALISM

Just as Essentialism is enjoying a revival, Perennialism is also experiencing a renaissance with the "Paideia proposal" designed by Mortimer Adler, a longtime associate of Robert Hutchins. Derived from the Greek, *paideia* refers to the "upbringing of children"; it signifies the general learning that all human beings should have. True to Perennialist principles, the Paideia proposal argues that a genuinely equal educational opportunity should be the same for all children; it should provide the "same quantity," "the same number of years" of schooling, and the "same quality of education."[7] The Paideia proponents argue that to divide students into tracks or to create special programs for some students but not for others is to deny the same quality of education for all.

Stressing the commonality of human nature, Paideia advocates do not propose that schooling be a leveling process that reduces the differences in human capacities to a common denominator. Education's ultimate goal, they assert, is to see that "human beings become educated persons."[8] Construed in Aristotelian terms, schooling not only provides skill and knowledge but also cultivates the habits or dispositions for lifelong education.

Schooling in the Paideia Proposal

For the Paideia proponents, the school, as an institution, provides a one-track rather than a multitrack system of education for all. The issue of a multitrack versus a single-track system raises complicated social, political, economic, and educational dimensions. Advocates of a multitrack system have varying motivations. Some believe that because of students' different intellectual capacities, socioeconomic backgrounds, and physiological–emotional needs, schools need to provide educational options to educate a widely differing student population. Still other advocates of multitrack education, including some Essentialists, believe that schools should sort students according to their academic abilities and should provide the intellectually gifted with a special kind of education that will prepare them as a leadership elite, especially a technological and scientific one. In contrast, Paideia proponents, like Perennialists in general, concentrate on the universality of human nature.

Schooling, according to Paideia proponents, has three major objectives common for all students: (1) it should provide the means of mental, moral, and spiritual growth; (2) it should cultivate the civic knowledge and virtues for responsible citizenship; (3) it should provide the basic skills needed for work rather than particular job training for a single occupation.[9]

Paideia proponents, like the Classical Realists treated in Chapter 3, warn against premature vocational training, which weakens or diminishes general education. Based on the liberal arts and sciences, all people should have a general education to cultivate their human nature and its undergirding rationality. Specialized vocational training, at the expense of general education, limits a person to one economic undertaking which can quickly become obsolete.

The Paideia Curriculum

Paideia advocates argue that all students should follow the same common curriculum for the twelve years of basic schooling. Students, however, would have a choice regarding their second language. The curriculum consists of three related but different learning modes, which have as their goals: (1) acquiring organized knowledge, (2) developing learning and intellectual skills, and (3) enlarging the understanding of ideas and values.[10]

For the acquisition of knowledge, the Paideia proponents, like the Essentialists and the Idealists, Realists, and Thomists, rely on organized subject matter. Their curriculum consists of language, literature, fine arts, mathematics, natural sciences, history, geography, and social studies.

To develop learning and intellectual skills, Paideia proponents emphasize basic skills such as "reading, writing, speaking, listening, observing, measuring, estimating, and calculating."[11] These skills are not taught in isolation but are integral to the entire curriculum. Again, a similarity exists in the identification of basic foundational skills between the Paideia proponents and the Essentialists, who see such skills as "generative" or necessary to other kinds of learning.

In the third area of curriculum, enlarging the understanding, the Paideia proponents return to a basic Perennialist theme—one long associated with Robert Hutchins and continued by Mortimer Adler—that the reading and discussion of the great books or classics are vital to the development of a truly educated person. In Adler's *The Paideia Proposal,* the scope of the great literature encompasses not only the enduring "historical, scientific, and philosophical" works but also the great works in film, drama, dance, and music.[12]

Teaching and Learning in the Paideia School

Teachers in schools following the Paideia theory of education are expected to be liberally educated persons. The methods used by such teachers correspond to the three branches of the curriculum. In teaching the organized subjects that lead to the acquisition of knowledge, the method used is essentially didactic, or instructional, using well-organized narratives. To instruct students to master the essential foundational skills, the teacher uses coaching, which refers to organizing and correcting students to perform skills such as reading or listening correctly. In studying the great works of art and literature that enlarge human understanding, teachers and students enter into the Socratic mode, which uses probing questions and directed discussions.

PERENNIALISM'S PHILOSOPHICAL AND IDEOLOGICAL RELATIONSHIPS

As indicated in earlier sections of this chapter, Perennialism exhibits strong affinities with Realism, especially its classical and Thomistic variations. (See Chapters 3 and 4 for a discussion of these philosophies.) In its curricular orientation and stress on fundamental or essential skills and subjects, it also resembles Essentialism, discussed in Chapter 17. Perennialism has several characteristics that distinguish it from Essentialism, however. Perennialism is distinctively Aristotelian, especially in its assertion that human beings are defined by their essential rationality, which is their universal character. American Perennialism also has been shaped by the strong imprint of Robert Hutchins and the "great books" program and Mortimer Adler's Paideia proposal and program. Although Perennialism, in Western Europe and the United States, has been shaped largely by educators influenced by Aristotelian and Thomist Realism, its principles would also be compatible with Idealism's emphasis on universal truth and values. The Idealist preference for the classics is also highly compatible with Perennialism.

Because of its Aristotelian and Realist origins, Perennialism differs from Naturalism, Pragmatism, and Existentialism, examined in Chapters 5, 6, and 7. Unlike Rousseau and other Naturalists, Perennialists give priority to cultivating human rationality through the great works of art, literature, and science. The Perennialist reliance on these great works of Western civilization as a basis for the curriculum differs from the Naturalist emphasis on instincts, feelings, and direct experience. While Perennialists would find much to admire in John Dewey's emphasis on shared experience, they would disagree with the Pragmatist's reliance on the scientific method, stress on change and relativity, and rejection of absolute truths. To the extent that Progressivism (discussed in Chapter 19) neglects foundational skills and the great literary and scientific achievements of the past, Perennialism would oppose it.

Perennialists would agree with certain aspects of Existentialism. They would agree, for example, that human beings should be free to define their projects in order to achieve self-realization. However, Perennialism has an antecedent definition of human beings as rational. Based on this definition, they encourage a sameness or uniformity in the curriculum designed to cultivate their conception of rationality. Existentialists, however, would find this a prior definition that limits human choice and freedom. Perennialists would counter that genuine choice is based on the human power to use knowledge to frame alternatives.

Just as Essentialism has been revived as an educational theory compatible with Neo-Conservatism, Perennialism, too, has enjoyed a renascence. While Essentialism has been used to support arguments for basic skills and subjects that are useful for economic growth, Perennialism's contemporary popularity rests with its emphasis on universal truth and values and its rejection of relativism. Both contemporary Essentialists and Perennialists decry the erosion of academic standards. Perennialists carry the argument further by contending that general intellectual and ethical standards have also eroded because of relativism. For example, Allan Bloom's *The Closing of the American Mind* argued forcefully that relativism in higher education had seriously weakened Americans' sense of intellectual and moral judgment.[13]

Lynne Cheney has argued against relativism in education by asserting that models of excellence in history and literature rest on truths that transcend time and circumstance. These objective truths, which transcend class, race, and gender, are appropriate to all human beings.[14] It is necessary to protect these models of objective truth and value against those who would subvert and use them as ideological tools. Deconstructionists and other postmodern theorists are among those subverting models and standards of objective truth. These critics of universalist standards contend that what is claimed to be objective truth is really a construction of dominant historical and contemporary groups. They argue that the constructed canon in philosophy, literature, and history can be deconstructed and analyzed in terms of its genesis and implication for gender, race, and class descrimination.

Perennialists claim that their educational theory is rooted in universal concepts of truth and justice and is not subservient to any particular ideology. They reject an ideological foundation for education since ideology is tied to particular social, political, and economic contexts, to the contingencies of human culture, rather than its universal character. Claiming that education is designed to cultivate the essential character of a universal human nature, they argue that they can speak about human rights and freedom in universal terms that are transcultural and transnational. They contend that relativistic philosophies such as Pragmatism and educational theories such as Progressivism have weakened the possibility of a truly worldwide or global civilization because they deny the importance of universals. Further, Perennialists claim that Social Reconstructionism and Critical Theory, for example, seek to impose particular ideological frames of reference on education that would lead to political indoctrination.

Critical Theorists counter the Perennialist claim to nonideological purity. They argue that the stress on the great classic books of Western civilization recommended by Hutchins, for example, is really a product of a Eurocentric ideological bias that represents the imposition of the ideology of the dominant culture. Both Reconstructionists and Critical Theorists also contend that the Perennialists' alleged universality is really a culturally based theoretical support of historically dominant institutions.

CONCLUSION

Perennialism asserts certain principles that are foundational to its educational directives. Among them are the following: (1) permanence is of a greater reality than change; (2) the universe is orderly and patterned; (3) the basic features of human nature reappear in each generation regardless of time or place; (4) human nature is universal in its essential characteristics; (5) like human nature, the basic goals of education are universal and timeless; (6) the human being's defining characteristic is rationality, which it is education's task to cultivate; and (7) the funded wisdom of the human race is recorded in certain classic works.

DISCUSSION QUESTIONS

1. Review Chapters 3 and 4. How does Perennialism resemble Realism and Thomism?

2. Define and explain the meaning of the term *Perennialism.*

3. Lead a discussion on one of the "great books" of Western civilization.

4. Debate the Perennialist assertion that vocational and career preparation should not be permitted to interfere with general education.

5. Debate the Perennialist assertion that all students should experience the same curriculum.

6. Does the Perennialist insistence on a common curriculum for all students enhance or retard equality of educational opportunity?

7. Critique Perennialism from the Naturalist and Pragmatist perspectives.

8. Is Perennialism anti-ideological or is it part of an ideological perspective?

9. What trends in society and education would Perennialists identify as eroding standards and values?

INQUIRY PROJECTS

- Read and review a book on education written by Robert Hutchins.
- Read and review a book on education written by Jacques Maritain.
- Using the Perennialist criteria, compile a reading list of the "great books."
- If there is a school in your locality that has adopted the Paideia program, visit it and observe instruction. Report on your observations to the class.
- Read and review a book on the Paideia proposal and program.
- In a character sketch, prepare a paper that describes a Paideia teacher.
- Using one of the "great books," lead a discussion on its important principles.
- Review several of the books being used in the teacher education program at your college or university. Do the authors of these books emphasize universal values or cultural relativism?

FURTHER READINGS

Adler, Mortimer J. *Paideia Problems and Possibilities: A Consideration of Questions Raised by the Paideia Proposal.* New York: Macmillan, 1983.

Adler, Mortimer J. *The Paideia Program: An Educational Syllabus.* New York: Macmillan, 1984.

Adler, Mortimer J. *The Paideia Proposal: An Educational Manifesto.* New York: Macmillan, 1982.

Ashmore, Harry S. *Unseasonable Truths: The Life of Robert Maynard Hutchins.* Boston: Little, Brown, 1991.

Bloom, Allan. *The Closing of the American Mind.* New York: Simon & Schuster, 1987.

Cheney, Lynne V. *Humanities in America: A Report to the President, the Congress, and the American People.* Washington, DC: National Endowment for the Humanities, 1988.

Cheney, Lynne V. *Telling the Truth.* New York: Simon & Schuster, 1995.

Dawson, Christopher. *The Crisis of Western Education.* New York: Sheed & Ward, 1961.

Dawson, Christopher. *The Historic Reality of Christian Culture.* New York: Harper & Brothers, 1960.

Dzuback, Mary Ann. *Robert M. Hutchins: Portrait of an Educator.* Chicago: University of Chicago Press, 1991.

Hopkins, Martin L. *Historical Analysis of Experimentalism and Perennialism in American Education.* Pomona, CA: California State Polytechnic University, Teacher Preparation Center, 1986.

Hutchins, Robert Maynard. *Conflict in Education in a Democratic Society.* New York: Harper and Co., 1953.

Hutchins, Robert Maynard. *A Conversation on Education.* Santa Barbara, CA: Center for the Study of Democratic Institutions, 1963.

Hutchins, Robert Maynard. *Education for Freedom.* Baton Rouge: Louisiana State University Press, 1943.

Hutchins, Robert Maynard. *The Higher Learning in America.* New Haven, CT: Yale University Press, 1936.

Hutchins, Robert Maynard. *The Learning Society.* New York: Praeger, 1968.

Hutchins, Robert Maynard. *Some Observations on American Education.* Cambridge: Cambridge University Press, 1956.

Hutchins, Robert Maynard. *The University of Utopia.* Chicago: University of Chicago Press, 1953.

Klauder, Francis J. *A Philosophy Rooted in Love: The Dominant Themes in the Perennial Philosophy of St. Thomas Aquinas.* Lanham, MD: University Press of America, 1994.

Maritain, Jacques. *Challenges and Renewals.* Notre Dame, IN: Notre Dame University Press, 1966.

Maritain, Jacques. *Education at the Crossroads.* New Haven, CT: Yale University Press, 1943.

Maritain, Jacques. *Integral Humanism.* New York: Charles Scribner's Sons, 1968.

Maritain, Jacques. *Man and the State.* Chicago: University of Chicago Press, 1951.

McNeill, William H. *Hutchins's University: A Memoir of the University of Chicago, 1929–1950.* Chicago: University of Chicago Press, 1991.

ENDNOTES

1. For a discussion of Hutchins's work at the University of Chicago, see William H. McNeill, *Hutchins's University: A Memoir of the University of Chicago, 1929–1950* (Chicago: University of Chicago Press, 1991).

2. Biographies of Hutchins are Harry S. Ashmore, *Unseasonable Truths: The Life of Robert Maynard Hutchins* (Boston: Little, Brown, 1991); and Mary Ann Dzuback, *Robert M. Hutchins: Portrait of an Educator* (Chicago: University of Chicago Press, 1991).

3. Robert M. Hutchins, *A Conversation on Education* (Santa Barbara, CA: Center for the Study of Democratic Institutions, 1963), pp. 1–2.

4. Robert M. Hutchins, *The Higher Learning in America* (New Haven, CT: Yale University Press, 1936), p. 63.

5. Francis J. Klauder, *A Philosophy Rooted in Love: The Dominant Themes in the Perennial Philosophy of St. Thomas Aquinas* (Lanham, MD: University Press of America, 1994).

6. Jacques Maritain, *Education at the Crossroads* (New Haven, CT: Yale University Press, 1960), p. 10.

7. Mortimer J. Adler, *The Paideia Proposal: An Educational Manifesto* (New York: Macmillan, 1982), p. 4.

8. Ibid., p. 10.

9. Ibid., pp. 16–17.

10. Ibid., pp. 22–23.

11. Ibid., p. 26.

12. Ibid., pp. 28–29. Also see Mortimer J. Adler, *The Paideia Program: An Educational Syllabus* (New York: Macmillan, 1984).

13. Allan Bloom, *The Closing of the American Mind* (New York: Simon & Schuster, 1987).

14. For Cheney's ideas on education, see Lynne V. Cheney, *Humanities in America: A Report to the President, the Congress, and the American People* (Washington, DC: National Endowment for the Humanities, 1988); Lynne V. Cheney, *Telling the Truth* (New York: Simon & Schuster, 1995).

Chapter 3

Progressivism and Education

In its origins, Progressivism in U.S. education began as a reaction against the formalism, verbalism, and authoritarianism of traditional schooling. While the various phases and nuances of Progressivism will be developed later in the chapter, an initial definition of Progressivism is presented here. Progressivism is the orientation that believes that improvement and reform in the human condition and society are both possible and desirable. Many early Progressive educators were looking for educational innovations that would liberate the child's energies. Other Progressives, identified with John Dewey's Pragmatism, believed that schools were part of a larger framework of institutional and social reform. In the sections that follow, we examine the sources of Progressivism, William H. Kilpatrick's project method, Progressivism's professional impact, and Progressivism's philosophical and ideological relationships.

SOURCES OF PROGRESSIVISM

Although the Progressive Education Association was formally organized in 1919, its antecedents reach back to the eighteenth-century Enlightenment. Like the theorists of the Age of Reason, modern Progressives emphasized the concept of "Progress," which asserts that human beings are capable of improving and perfecting their environments by applying human intelligence and the scientific method to solving social, political, and economic problems. Like Rousseau, the Progressives rejected the doctrine of human depravity and believed that people were essentially benevolent.

Progressivism was also rooted in the spirit of social reform that gripped the early twentieth-century Progressive movement in U.S. politics. As a sociopolitical movement, Progressivism held that human society could be refashioned by political reforms. Such U.S. political programs as Woodrow Wilson's "New Freedom," Theodore Roosevelt's "New Nationalism," and Robert LaFollette's "Wisconsin Idea," although varied in particulars, shared the common concern that the emerging corporate society should be ordered to function democratically for the benefit of all Americans.[1] The leaders in Progressive politics represented what was essentially the middle-class orientation to reform characterized by gradual change through legislation and peaceful social innovation through education.

U.S. educational Progressives could also look to the major educational reformers of Western Europe for inspiration and stimulation. Jean-Jacques Rousseau, author of *Émile,* had written about an education that proceeded along natural lines and that was free of coercion. As an early rebel against traditional schooling, Rousseau argued that learning was most effective when it followed the child's interests and needs.

Progressives could also feel an affinity for the work of Johann Heinrich Pestalozzi, a nineteenth-century Swiss educational reformer, who, as a willing disciple of Rousseau, asserted that education should be more than book learning. It should embrace the whole child—emotions, intellect, and body. Natural education, said Pestalozzi, should take place in an environment of emotional love and security. It should also begin in the child's immediate environment and involve the operations of the senses on the objects found in the environment.[2]

The work of the Viennese psychoanalyst Sigmund Freud was also useful to Progressive educators. In examining cases of hysteria, Freud had traced some mental illnesses to early childhood traumas. He believed that authoritarian parents had caused many children to repress their drives. This repression, especially in the case of sexual drives, could lead to neurotic behavior that had a deleterious effect on the child and on his or her adult life.

While the European educational reformers provided stimulus for Progressive educators, it was John Dewey and his followers who came to exert a profound influence on Progressive education. It should be clear, however, that not all Progressives were Deweyites. Progressive education as a movement was a convenient platform, a rallying point, for those who opposed educational traditionalism rather than a doctrinaire movement.

The Progressive Educational Platform

Before commenting on John Dewey's reactions to Progressive education, a review of the history of Progressive education provides a perspective on the work of the Progressive educators. Certain educators, such as Flora Cooke, principal of the Francis W. Parker School in Chicago, and Carleton Washburne of the Winnetka, Illinois, Schools, had in the early twentieth century developed innovative methods that stressed the child's own initiative in learning. Junius L. Meriam of the University of Missouri had developed an activity curriculum that included excursions, constructive work, observation, and discussion. Marietta Johnson

(1864–1938) had also established the School of Organic Education in 1907 in Fairhope, Alabama. Johnson's Organic Theory of education emphasized the child's needs, interests, and activities. Special attention was given to creative activity that included dancing, sketching, drawing, singing, weaving, and other expressive activities. Formal instruction in reading, writing, and arithmetic was reserved until the child was nine or ten years old. The general method of instruction was that of the free-flowing discussion.

In 1919, a number of Progressive educators met in Washington, D.C., and organized the Progressive Education Association under the leadership of Stanwood Cobb, head of the Chevy Chase Country Day School. To give cohesion to the Progressive educational position, the association stressed the following principles: (1) Progressive education should provide the freedom that would encourage the child's natural development and growth through activities that cultivated his or her initiative, creativity, and self-expression; (2) all instruction should be guided by the child's own interest, stimulated by contact with the real world; (3) the Progressive teacher was to guide the child's learning as a director of research activities, rather than as a taskmaster; (4) student achievement was to be measured in terms of mental, physical, moral, and social development; (5) there should be greater cooperation among the teacher, the school, and the home and family in meeting the child's needs for growth and development; (6) the truly Progressive school should be a laboratory in innovative practices.[3]

At the onset, the Progressive Education Association as a child-centered movement was a reaction against the subject-matter curriculum of traditional schooling. It attracted teachers and parents associated with small, private experimental schools. In the 1920s and 1930s, the Progressive Education Association began to attract professional educators from colleges of education. Many of these educators had been influenced by John Dewey's Experimentalist philosophy of education.

Dewey's Critique of Progressive Education

Although John Dewey's Experimentalism has been discussed elsewhere in this book, the Progressive educational position is made clear by a brief examination of Dewey's critique of the movement, which appeared in *Experience and Education*.[4]

Dewey warned that the controversy between traditional and Progressive educators had tended to degenerate into an assertion of either/or positions. Although sympathetic to Progressivism, Dewey believed that many Progressives were merely reacting against traditional school practices and had failed to formulate an educational philosophy that was capable of serving as a plan of pragmatic operations.

Dewey's analysis of the traditional and the Progressive school is useful in highlighting the contrasts between these two institutions. The traditional school, he said, was a formal institution that emphasized a subject-matter curriculum comprised of discretely organized disciplines, such as language, history, mathematics, and science. Traditionalists, such as Perennialists and Essentialists, held that the source of wisdom was located in humanity's cultural heritage. Morals, standards, and conduct were derived from tradition and were not subject to the test of the scientific method. The traditional teacher regarded the written word as the font of wisdom and relied on the textbook as the source of knowledge and the recitation as the means of eliciting it from students. Traditionalists had attempted to isolate the school from social controversies. Holding to their belief that learning was the transmission and mastery of bodies of knowledge inherited from the past, the traditionalists had ignored the learner's own needs and interests and had deliberately neglected urgent social and political issues. The products of conventional education (namely, the students) were expected to be receptive of the traditional wisdom, have habits and attitudes that were conducive to conformity, and were to be respectful of and obedient to authority.

Although Dewey shared the Progressive antagonism toward the traditional school, he feared that many Progressives were merely reacting against it. Too many Progressives had ignored the past and were concerned only with the present. In their opposition to the traditional school's passivity, some Progressives had come to emphasize any kind of activity, even purposeless activity. Many Progressives had become so antagonistic to education imposed by adults that they had begun to cater to childish whims, many of which were devoid of social and intellectual value.

After urging that Progressive educators avoid the polarization of an either/ or educational position, Dewey outlined the philosophy that he believed was suited for the genuinely Progressive school. Progressive education needed a philosophy based on experience, the interaction of the person with the environment. Such an experiential philosophy was to have no set of external goals. Rather, the end product of education was growth—that ongoing experience which leads to the direction and control of subsequent experience.

Truly Progressive education should not ignore the past but rather should use it to reconstruct experience in the present and direct future experiences. For Dewey, education should be based on a continuum of ongoing experience that united the past and the present and led to the shaping of the future.

Dewey also warned that Progressive education should not become so absorbed in activity that it misconstrued the nature of activity. Mere movement was without value. Activity should be directed to solving problems; it should be purposeful and should contain social and intellectual possibilities that contributed to the learner's growth.

The true Progressive educator was a teacher skilled in relating the learner's internal conditions of experience—that is, the student's needs, interests, purposes, capacities, and desires—with the objective conditions of experience—the environmental factors that were historical, physical, economic, and sociological.

Dewey asserted that Progressivism should be free from a naive romanticization of child nature. Although children's interests and needs were always at the beginning of learning, they were not its end. The child's instincts and impulses needed to be refined and developed into reflective social intelligence. Some impulses contained possibilities for growth and development; other impulses would have the opposite result in that their consequences would impede such growth. Impulse became reflective when the learner was able to estimate the consequences of acting on it. By developing an "end-in-view," the learner could conjecture the consequences that would result from action. Understanding the purpose of a particular act involved estimating the consequences that had occurred in similar situations in the past and forming a tentative judgment about the likely consequences of acting in the present. Thus, Progressive education should encourage the cultivation of purposeful, reflective patterns of inquiry in the learner.

Challenging Essentialism and Perennialism, Dewey warned educators against trying to "return to the intellectual methods and ideals that arose centuries before scientific method was developed." Truly Progressive educators would seek systematically to utilize the "scientific method as the pattern and ideal of intelligent exploration and exploitation of the potentialities inherent in experience."[5]

WILLIAM KILPATRICK AND THE PROJECT METHOD

Dewey's plea for a Progressive education based on human experience stimulated William Heard Kilpatrick (1871–1965), who was both an Experimentalist and a Progressive, to construct a methodology of instruction that united purpose and activity and that tested conjectured consequences in action. Kilpatrick, a popular professor at Columbia University's Teachers College, devised the "project method" that came to characterize Progressive education for many U.S. educators.

A brief discussion of Kilpatrick's route to the development of the project method is useful in understanding the Progressive impulse among U.S. educators. Born in rural White Plains, Georgia, the son of a Baptist minister, Kilpatrick received a traditional education. After attending Mercer University, he taught algebra and geometry in the public schools of Blakely in his native state.[6]

As a mathematics teacher, Kilpatrick inaugurated reforms in his classroom. For example, he believed that report cards and grades focused attention on extrinsic rewards that were disconnected from the natural consequences of learning. He abolished the practice of external marks, which he felt encouraged egotism among the achievers and inflicted a sense of inferiority on slower learners. In cultivating freedom in his classroom, he encouraged his students to work collaboratively. Early in his career Kilpatrick revealed a liberal attitude toward classroom discipline, which would later be more theoretically and systematically organized in his project method.

In 1907, Kilpatrick entered Teachers College at Columbia University to continue his professional and academic preparation in education. Here he encountered and accepted John Dewey's pragmatic philosophy.

Later, as a professor of education at Teachers College, Kilpatrick became a noted interpreter of Dewey. His writings and lectures, which espoused themes associated with Experimentalist philosophy and Progressive education, attracted a large and receptive audience. A gifted lecturer, Kilpatrick clarified many of Dewey's more difficult theoretical concepts, He was not, however, merely an interpreter. He also advanced his own educational philosophy, which synthesized Progressivism and Experimentalism into the "purposeful act," or the "project method."[7] Because he reached a large number of teachers in his classes, Kilpatrick exerted a shaping influence over U.S. educational theory and practice.

Kilpatrick's project method rejected traditional education's reliance on a book-centered instruction. Although not an anti-intellectual, Kilpatrick asserted that books were not a substitute for learning through living. The most pernicious form of bookishness was found in the textbook's domination of conventional teaching. Too frequently, teachers relied exclusively on information in textbooks. This often led to mechanically organized, secondhand experiences. The student who succeeded in the traditional school was frequently of a bookish inclination and successful in memorizing but not always in understanding what was read. Because of its stress on bookishness and memorization, conventional schooling had degenerated into devitalized mechanical routines in which teachers assigned lessons from textbooks, drilled their students on the assignments, heard recitations of memorized responses, and then evaluated them on their recall of the material. Such schooling, in Kilpatrick's view, stifled individual creativity, led to boredom, and lacked collaborative social purposes.

In contrast to the rote nature of traditional book-centered education, Kilpatrick's project method was designed to elaborate a constructive Progressivism along Experimentalist lines. In the project method, students were to choose, plan, direct, and execute their work in activities, or projects, that would stimulate purposeful efforts. In its theoretical formulation, the project was a mode of problem solving. Students, either individually or in groups, would define problems that arose in their own experiences. Learning would be task centered in that success would come by solving the problem and testing the solution by acting on it. Action from purposeful planning would meet the pragmatic test and be judged by its consequences.

Kilpatrick recommended that the school curriculum be organized into four major classes of projects. First, the creative, or "construction," project involved concretizing a theoretical plan in external form. For example, the students might decide to write and then present a drama. They would write the script, assign the roles, and actually act out the play. Or, the creative project might actually involve the design of a blueprint for a library. The test would come in the construction of the library from the plan devised by the students. Second, the appreciation, or "enjoyment," project was designed to contribute to aesthetic enjoyment. Reading a novel, seeing a film, or hearing a symphony were examples of projects that would lead to aesthetic appreciation. Third, the "problem" project was one in which the students would be involved in resolving an intellectual problem. Such problems as the resolution of racial discrimination, the improvement of the quality of the environment, or the organization of recreational facilities were social problems that called for disciplined intellectual inquiry. Finally, the "specific learning" project involved the acquiring of a skill or an area of knowledge. Learning to type, swim, dance, read, or write were examples of the acquisition of a specific skill.

Kilpatrick's project method should be interpreted both in terms of its suggested social consequences and its strictly educational aims. To be sure, the project method had educational objectives, such as improvement in creative, constructive, appreciative, intellectual, and skill competencies. However, acquiring these competencies was only a part of Kilpatrick's plan for educational reform. Kilpatrick believed, as did Dewey, that education as a social activity was a product of human association and collaboration. In a free society, democratic discussion, debate, decision, and action depended on the willingness of individuals to use the methods of open and uncoerced inquiry. Kilpatrick believed that the project method lent itself to group work, in which students could collaboratively pursue common problems and share in associative inquiry. Such was the essence of the democratic processes. Even more important than the acquiring of specific skills was the student's need to acquire attitudes appropriate to a democratic society.

The person that Kilpatrick envisioned as a result of education based on purposeful collaboration was the democratic man or woman. Such a person would possess an experimental attitude and would be willing to test inherited traditions, values, and beliefs. Through the project method, students would learn to use democratic methods of open discussion, carefully reasoned deliberation, decision making that respected both the rights of the majority and the minority, and action that resulted in peaceful social change.

Kilpatrick's model of the democratic citizen was much like that envisioned by the middle-class Progressives in politics and in education.[8] This person would use a democratic methodology and would expect opponents to use the same procedure. As a reconstructive person, this Progressively educated man or woman would believe that social institutions were creations of human intelligence and could be periodically renovated when the situation required it. The democratic citizen would be open to using the scientific method and would discard theological, metaphysical, political, and economic absolutes as dogmatic impediments that blocked human inquiry into the conditions of life. Above all, Kilpatrick wanted to educate individuals who shared a common framework of democratic values. Such men and women would be wholehearted and willing participants in the democratic community.

PROGRESSIVISM'S PROFESSIONAL IMPACT

As indicated, Progressive educators such as Kilpatrick sought to reconceptualize the U.S. school curriculum and methods of instruction along more open-ended, experimental, and collaborative lines.[9] However, the degree to which Progressive education actually was felt in educational practice has been much debated. Historians such as Cremin argue that certain Progressive educational innovations became so commonplace in the schools that they no longer appeared to be reforms. Critics of Progressivism, such as Essentialists, Perennialists, and Neo-Conservatives, have argued that Progressivism exercised a pervasive but deleterious influence on public schools in that it contributed to the lowering of academic standards and achievement.

Arthur Zilversmit, in *Changing Schools,* posed the question, Did Progressive philosophy actually impact educational policy and practices in local schools? He argues that the impact of any educational philosophy, including Progressivism, needs to be assessed in terms of U.S. public schooling's basic organizational reality. Public schools are local agencies, governed by local boards of education, administered by local superintendents, and taught by teachers who serve local populations. For Zilversmit, the impact of Progressivism must be assessed in terms of local personalities, their social and educational attitudes, and available community resources. While Progressivism had an impact on schools, Zilversmit found that it was more eclectic and less systematic than was generally assumed. According to his analysis, some Progressive educators inaugurated curricular and methodological reforms while others, primarily school administrators, emphasized efficiency, effectiveness, and economical organization, structures, and scheduling. Indeed, Winnetka's superintendent, Carleton Washburne, was a Progressive exemplar who competently blended curricular and administrative Progressivism.[10]

Progressivism entered schools eclectically in the administration of superintendents who were professionally prepared in what was called the "modern" philosophy of education. Concurrent with the Progressive movement and Progressive ideology, the modern, as contrasted with the traditional, philosophy selectively incorporated Progressive principles. The modern philosophy of education was an essential feature of many university programs of professional education. In the modern approach, key features were (1) larger schools facilitating more class sections and more curriculum diversity; (2) curriculum diversity enhancing educational enrichment; and (3) a propensity to create junior high or middle schools as distinct schools. These features were often endorsed by Progressives and became part of the modern school administrator's ideology.[11]

In addition to its eclectic implementation in schools, Progressivism influenced the educational profession, especially in its professional organizations and journals. In the case of U.S. educational philosophy, its origins coincided with the more general Progressive movement. Kaminsky, in *A New History of Educational Philosophy,* relates the origins of educational philosophy to reformist tendencies that provided a critique of "America's version of Victorianism."[12] Progressives took the lead in the American Social Science Association to free social inquiry from metaphysically based formal constraints. Dewey and other Progressive intellectuals worked to make educational philosophy a weapon of social and educational reform against Herbert Spencer's entrenched Social Darwinism.

Progressives were members of a complex and interlocking network of professional organizations such as the National Educational Association, the Progressive Education Association, the John Dewey Society, and the Philosophy of Education Society, and published in professional journals such as *Progressive Education, The Social Frontier,* and *Educational Theory.*[13]

The Progressive Teacher

Progressive education called for a teacher who was different in temperament, training, and techniques from teachers in more traditional schools. Although the Progressive teacher needed to be competent in the content and methods of inquiry of such academic disciplines as history, science, mathematics, and language, instruction in the Progressive classroom required more than a chronological or a systematic subject-matter presentation of the various learned disciplines. The Progressive approach was interdisciplinary. Problems were not specifically located within a particular learned discipline but rather intersected them in interdisciplinary fashion.

Because the Progressive classroom was oriented to purposeful activity, the Progressive teacher needed to know how to motivate the students so that they initiated, planned, and carried out their projects. As learning was centered in the participating group, the Progressive teacher needed to know how to use collaborative processes.

Perhaps the most difficult challenge for the teacher was to act as a guide rather than the center of learning. The skilled teacher, in the Progressive context, did not dominate the classroom as its focal point. Rather, he or she made the interests of the learner central. The teacher was properly a guide to discussing, planning, and executing learning.

PROGRESSIVISM'S PHILOSOPHICAL AND IDEOLOGICAL RELATIONSHIPS

As a theory of education, Progressivism draws heavily from the philosophies of Naturalism, examined in Chapter 5, and Pragmatism, examined in Chapter 6. From Naturalists, such as Rousseau, Progressives borrowed the doctrine that children should be free to develop according to their interests and needs. As indicated, the Experimentalists who were part of the Progressive persuasion disagreed when the child-centered Progressives exaggerated children's interests to the point of ignoring or discounting the educative role of society.

The child-centered Progressives' emphasis on children's needs and interests led them to conclude that the curriculum should develop from the child and that the most effective school environment was a permissive one in which children were free to explore and act on their interests. From the origins of Progressivism to the present, Progressives have stressed children's directly expressed needs and interests over academic subject matter.

While some Progressives were influenced by Naturalism, others drew their educational rationale from the Pragmatism or Experimentalism of John Dewey. Although they could agree that children should be liberated from repressive schooling, they disagreed on the extent to which education was a social force or involved some degree of social imposition. Believing that human intelligence was shaped by social interaction, Deweyan Progressives gave a greater role to the group and to social issues and problems. Deweyan Progressives also emphasized the power of the scientific method to achieve complete and reflective thought. Deweyan Progressives would see Rousseau's isolation of the child from society and complete reliance on the child's freedom to be a romanticization of the child's nature and an abandonment of the educator's social responsibility. Thus, Progressivism's philosophical reliance on both Naturalism and Pragmatism has caused internal tensions.

Progressivism rejects the more traditional philosophies of Idealism, Realism, and Thomism and their emphasis on antecedent reality, hierarchical categories, and subject matter. It should be pointed out, however, that the Idealist emphasis on child growth, exemplified in Froebel's kindergarten, was an early influence on many Progressives. Moreover, the Idealist concern for social integration had an impact on Dewey's thought.

Ideologically, Progressivism is most compatible with Liberalism, in both its classical and more modern forms, than with other ideologies. Liberalism's concern for individual rights and freedom finds an educational corollary in Progressivism's emphasis on the individual child. The freedom to inquire and test ideas, exemplified by Liberal theorists such as John Stuart Mill, is also stressed by Progressives.

The Progressive inclination toward change rather than stasis is much like the Liberal orientation. Progressivism is seen by Conservatives as threatening cultural continuity, eroding the power of tradition as a stabilizing factor, and jeopardizing legitimate authority. Conservatives fear that Progressive permissiveness, like Liberal individualism, will weaken standards.

The Liberal emphasis on representative institutions and gradual incremental reform rather than sweeping Utopian grand designs or Marxist revolution is compatible with Progressive social reform. Progressive social reformers such as Jane Addams, Woodrow Wilson, and Theodore Roosevelt worked within the social and political system. Their efforts at reform were designed to improve the system by using representative institutions and processes to remedy its internal weaknesses. Progressive reformers, like Liberals in general, prefer open-ended reform, which has limited ends-in-view rather than the preconceived ends found in both Utopian and Marxist ideologies.

Deweyan Progressives, while sharing many Liberal attitudes, reject the competitive ethic associated with Classical Liberalism and Social Darwinism. The old Liberalism was judged to be personally egotistical and socially and economically wasteful by Dewey, who condemned it and called for a new Liberalism that encouraged cooperation, social planning, and scientifically directed human experience.

Progressivism, like Experimentalism and Liberalism, is incompatible with both political and social totalitarianism and with the authoritarianism in education that flows from it. The Progressive emphasis on freedom to follow one's interests violates the totalitarian requirement that subordinates individual interests to the will of the leader or to the dictates of the state or party. The Progressive emphasis on experimentation and the testing of ideas and values in experience encourages a questioning attitude that is contrary to the totalitarian rule for unquestioning obedience.

Progressivism, as a theory of education, opposes many of the concepts and practices associated with Essentialism and Perennialism. The points of disagreement become clear by contrasting the positions of the basic educator and the Progressive educator. The basic educator, whose pedagogical position reflects the more traditional and conservative Essentialism and Perennialism, advocates the following:

1. Learning the general cultural tool skills that are foundational to other kinds of learning. For example, reading, writing, and arithmetic are identified as basic, foundational, and generative of other school subjects and out-of-school activities. Early on, the advocates of basic education construe schooling to be literary and book centered.

2. Organizing the curriculum around well-defined essential skills and subject matters. There is a general opposition to ill-defined, undifferentiated, and amorphous curricular patterns that emphasize open education, learning through field experiences, projects, activities, and other unstructured kinds of learning.

3. Identifying the school, its administrators, and teachers as academic experts who have knowledge of content and of instructional methods. The basic education proponent opposes using the school as a vehicle for social change, innovation, and experimentation. The classroom is dominated by the teacher and instruction is planned and directed by the teacher.

The Progressive educator, in contrast, takes the following pedagogical posture:

1. Rather than introducing basic skills directly, it is better to have children acquire methods of learning and investigating by solving their problems and satisfying their needs. For example, John Dewey argued that children learned to think by using the scientific method to solve problems. William Heard Kilpatrick stressed learning by means of collaborative activities in his project method. In other words, learning, the curriculum, and instruction come from the child's interests.

2. The school should be immersed in social issues and in advancing social change. Externally, school administrators and teachers should break down

the theoretical and political walls that separate the school from society. They should also demolish the inner walls of school organization that divide it into subject areas, grade levels, and departments.

3. Teachers should be project directors, stimulators of learning, counselors, and learning consultants rather than transmitters of information. Instruction should be varied and often indirect.

CONCLUSION

Progressive education urges the liberation of the child from a pedagogical tradition that emphasizes rote learning, lesson recitations, and textbook authority. In opposition to the conventional subject-matter disciplines of the traditional curriculum, Progressives seek to develop alternative modes of curricular organization. They encourage such varied but related alternatives as activities, experiences, problem solving, and the project method. Progressive education is characterized by (1) a focus on the child as the learner rather than on subject matter, (2) an emphasis on activities and experiences that are direct rather than an exclusive reliance on verbal and literary skills and knowledge, (3) the encouragement of collaborative group-learning activities rather than competitive individualized lesson learning. In its broad social directions, Progressivism in education encourages democratic procedures designed to create community participation and social reform. It also cultivates a cultural or ethical relativism that critically appraises and often rejects inherited traditions, attitudes, and values.

DISCUSSION QUESTIONS

1. Identify and analyze the sources of Progressivism in terms of their theoretical compatibility and internal consistency.

2. Compare and contrast the traditional and the Progressive schools.

3. Compare and contrast the Progressive and Conservative views of the past and their applications to instruction.

4. Using Kilpatrick's project method as a case study, analyze how theory is formulated from practice.

5. Identify the elements in Kilpatrick's project method that are derived from either Naturalism or Pragmatism.

6. Review Essentialism treated in Chapter 17. Using the Essentialist preference for differentiated learning, critique Kilpatrick's project method.

7. Using the Neo-Marxist concept of the "hidden curriculum," examine Kilpatrick's project method.

8. Compare and contrast the Progressive and basic education (Essentialist and Perennialist) conceptions of curriculum and instruction.

INQUIRY PROJECTS

- Prepare a paper that identifies and analyzes the antecedents of Progressivism.
- Prepare a biographical sketch of a Progressive educator such as Francis Parker, Jane Addams, Carleton Washburne, Junius Meriam, Marietta Johnson, William Heard Kilpatrick, or Harold Rugg.
- Based on the principles of Progressive education, prepare a character sketch of a Progressive teacher.
- Review Lawrence Cremin's *The Transformation of the School: Progressivism in American Education.*
- Review John Dewey's *Experience and Education.*
- Devise and prepare a lesson plan based on Kilpatrick's project method.
- Visit a school that embodies Progressive methods in its program. Report your observations to the class.
- Review national reports on education such as *A Nation at Risk* and *Action for Excellence.* Do these reports reflect an anti-Progressive point of view?

FURTHER READINGS

Blum, John M. *The Progressive Presidents: Roosevelt, Wilson, Roosevelt, Johnson.* New York: W. W. Norton, 1982.

Cremin, Lawrence A. *The Transformation of the School: Progressivism in American Education, 1876–1957.* New York: Alfred A. Knopf, 1961.

Crunden, Robert M. *Ministers of Reform: The Progressives' Achievement in American Civilization, 1889–1920.* Urbana: University of Illinois Press, 1984.

Dewey, John. *Experience and Education.* New York: Collier Books, 1963.

Graham, Patricia A. *Progressive Education: From Arcady to Academe: A History of the Progressive Education Association, 1919–1955.* New York: Teachers College Press, 1967.

Kaminsky, James S. *A New History of Educational Philosophy.* Westport, CT: Greenwood Press, 1993.

Kilpatrick, William H. *Education for a Changing Civilization.* New York: Macmillan, 1925.

Kilpatrick, William H. *The Foundations of Method.* New York: Macmillan, 1925.

Kilpatrick, William H. *Philosophy of Education.* New York: Macmillan, 1951.

Kilpatrick, William H. *The Project Method.* New York: Teachers College Press, 1921.

Kliebard, Herbert M. *The Struggle for the American Curriculum, 1893–1958.* Boston: Routledge & Kegan Paul, 1986.

Lauderdale, William B. *Progressive Education: Lessons from Three Schools.* Bloomington, IN: Phi Delta Kappa Educational Foundation, 1981.

Pratt, Caroline. *I Learn from Children.* New York: Simon & Schuster, 1948.

Ravitch, Diane. *The Troubled Crusade: American Education, 1945–1980.* New York: Basic Books, 1983.

Reese, William J. *Power and the Promise of School Reform: Grassroots Movements During the Progressive Era.* Boston: Routledge & Kegan Paul, 1986.

Rugg, Harold O., and Ann Schumaker. *The Child-Centered School.* New York: World Book Co., 1928.

Tanner, Daniel. *Crusade for Democracy: Progressive Education at the Cross-* roads. Albany: State University of New York Press, 1991.

Tenenbaum, Samuel. *William Heard Kilpatrick: Trail Blazer in Education.* New York: Harper and Brothers, 1951.

Washburne, Carleton. *What Is Progressive Education?* New York: John Day, 1952.

Zilversmit, Arthur. *Changing Schools: Progressive Education Theory and Practice, 1930–1960.* Chicago: University of Chicago Press, 1993.

ENDNOTES

1. For a discussion of Progressivism in U.S. politics, see John Morton Blum, *The Progressive Presidents: Roosevelt, Wilson, Roosevelt, Johnson* (New York: W. W. Norton, 1982).

2. For a discussion of Pestalozzi's educational theory and its significance for Progressivism, see Gerald L. Gutek, *Pestalozzi and Education* (New York: Random House, 1968).

3. For the definitive treatment of the Progressive Education Association, see Patricia Albjerg Graham, *Progressive Education: From Arcady to Academe—A History of the Progressive Education Association, 1919–1955* (New York: Teachers College Press, Columbia University, 1967); the definitive history of Progressive Education in the context of U.S. Progressivism can be found in Lawrence A. Cremin, *The Transformation of the School: Progressivism in American Education, 1876–1957* (New York: Alfred A. Knopf, 1961).

4. John Dewey, *Experience and Education* (New York: Collier Books, 1963).

5. Ibid., pp. 85–86.

6. For a study of Kilpatrick's life, educational philosophy, and influence, see Samuel Tenenbaum, *William Heard Kil-* patrick: *Trail Blazer in Education* (New York: Harper and Brothers, 1951).

7. William Heard Kilpatrick, "The Project Method," *Teachers College Record,* XIX (1918): 319–335, and *The Project Method* (New York: Teachers College Press, 1921).

8. For a discussion of middle-class Progressivism, see Robert M. Crunden, *Ministers of Reform: The Progressive's Achievement in American Civilization, 1889–1920* (Urbana: University of Illinois Press, 1984).

9. Herbert M. Kliebard, *The Struggle for the American Curriculum, 1893–1958* (Boston: Routledge & Kegan Paul, 1986).

10. Arthur Zilversmit, *Changing Schools: Progressive Education Theory and Practice, 1930–1960* (Chicago: University of Chicago Press, 1993), pp. 38–56.

11. Ibid., pp. 168–183.

12. James S. Kaminsky, *A New History of Educational Philosophy* (Westport, CT: Greenwood Press, 1993), pp. 19–23.

13. For a history of the John Dewey Society, see Daniel Tanner, *Crusade for Democracy: Progressive Education at the Crossroads* (Albany: State University of New York Press, 1991).

Chapter 4

Social Reconstructionism and Education

Social Reconstructionism sharply contrasts with the conservative Essentialist and Perennialist theories, which Reconstructionists regard to be reflective theories that mirror inherited social patterns and values. Reconstructionists assert that educators should originate policies and programs to reform society. Teachers, they say, should use their power to lead the young in programs of social engineering and reform.

Social Reconstructionists claim to follow John Dewey's Pragmatism, which emphasized the need to reconstruct both personal and social experience. Seizing on Dewey's emphasis on reconstructing experience, Reconstructionists stress the reconstruction of social experience and the culture.[1]

Although Social Reconstructionists differ on particulars, they agree on premises such as the following: (1) all philosophies, ideologies, and theories, including educational ones, are culturally based and emerge from specific cultural patterns that are conditioned by living at a given time and in a particular place; (2) culture, as a dynamic process, is growing and changing; and (3) human beings can refashion culture so that it promotes human growth and development.[2]

Rather than being abstract or based on speculative philosophy, educational theories, Reconstructionists contend, should shape social and political policies. Reconstructionists are suspicious of universalist or cosmic theories of education that emphasize highly abstract categories of unchanging reality, human nature, truth, and value. This suspicion can be traced to their Pragmatist origins and their rejection of the dualism found in Realism and Thomism and the educational theories derived from them, Perennialism and Essentialism.

Social Reconstructionists view contemporary society as facing a severe crisis resulting from humankind's unwillingness to reconstruct institutions and values to meet the needs of modern life. Human beings entered the modern technological and scientific era with attitudes and values derived from the rural, preindustrial past. To resolve the crisis, human beings need to examine their heritage and identify the viable elements that will help to resolve the present crisis. If people examine their heritage, deliberately plan the direction of change, and implement the plan, they can create a new social order. The school's task is to examine the cultural heritage critically and to emphasize the elements that can be used in the needed reconstruction of society. In the sections that follow, we examine cultural crisis and reconstruction; the pioneering work of George S. Counts; development theory and futurism; and issue-oriented schools; and consider Reconstructionism in its philosophical and ideological relationships.

CULTURAL CRISIS

Reconstructionism asserts that modern society is experiencing a profound crisis caused by an unwillingness to engage in fundamental cultural reconstruction. The symptoms of cultural crisis are many. There are great variations in economic levels of life, both in the United States and throughout the world. While a few people enjoy wealth, the vast majority struggle at a subsistence level that borders on dire poverty. In the United States, large numbers of people, especially members of minority groups, have been victimized by decades of poverty and discrimination. Internationally, two-thirds of the world's population is barely surviving. The Reconstructionist regards the contradiction between wealth and poverty as a residue of the prescientific past.

The world is plagued by international tensions and war or the threat of war. In an age of potential nuclear destruction, military conflict with the threat of escalation into worldwide holocaust jeopardizes humankind's continued existence on this planet. Further, the Reconstructionists point to myriad unresolved conflicts and to the wastage of human potential. Such problems as overpopulation, environmental pollution, violence, and terrorism are symptoms of the pervasive crisis.

At the root of the crisis is the severing of human values from social and economic realities. The human creative genius has developed dynamic scientific and technological instruments that contribute to further change. At the same time that the dynamic forces of science and technology have changed the material environment, an inherited conception of an idealized past seeks to preserve the status quo. While Reconstructionists examine the past to find viable elements in the cultural heritage that can be used instrumentally, they disdain theories that urge us to go back to the "good old days." For them, the nostalgia for a problem-free past is often an ideological camouflage used by Neo-Conservatives to preserve the status quo.

Cultural Reconstruction

Reconstructionists believe that modern society and human survival are intimately related. To ensure human survival and to create a more humane civilization, human beings need to become social engineers who can plan the course of change and use science and technology to achieve desired goals. Hence, Reconstructionist education should cultivate (1) a critical examination of the cultural heritage, (2) a commitment to work for deliberate social reform, (3) a planning attitude capable of plotting the course of cultural revision, and (4) the testing of the cultural plan by enacting programs of deliberate social reform.

Reconstructionists believe that all social reform arises in existing life conditions. Students are expected to define the major problems facing humankind and to recognize the dynamic forces of the present. Students should be able to detect the customs, beliefs, and values that impede social reconstruction. Values that are merely customary should be reconstructed. The moral and ideological culture is permeated with residues of the prescientific and pretechnological age. Customary and stereotypical ways of thinking that lead to intolerance, discrimination, and superstition should be identified and discarded.

THE PIONEERING WORK OF GEORGE S. COUNTS

A clear statement of the need for educators to resolve social problems was made by George S. Counts in his book *Dare the School Build a New Social Order?* George S. Counts (1889–1974) was an educator who stimulated Social Reconstructionist theory. Born in rural Kansas, Counts witnessed the geographical closing of the American frontier and believed that new frontiers needed to be forged in human ideas and social institutions. Counts, who earned his doctorate at the University of Chicago in 1916, applied social theory to educational issues. During his active life, Counts was a professor of education at Columbia University's Teachers College, a president of the American Federation of Teachers, a leader of New York's Liberal Party, and a determined advocate of civil liberties. He was also a distinguished comparative educator who developed pioneering insights into Soviet society and education. Although Counts was on the radical cutting edge of social change in the United States, he became a determined anti-Communist. He early detected the totalitarianism inherent in Stalinism in the Soviet Union.[3]

Although Counts did not formally identify with those who called themselves Social Reconstructionists, an analysis of his educational theory clarifies themes of central concern for Reconstructionist educators. Counts's still unanswered question—"Dare the school build a new social order?"—created a ferment that continues today.

A photograph of George S. Counts (1889–
1974), author of *Dare the School Build a New
Social Order?* and a leading Reconstructionist
theorist.

For Counts, the great crises of the twentieth century were symptoms of profound transition and rapid change. Acute cultural change occurred as U.S. society
moved between two very different social patterns. The older, agrarian, rural,
neighborhood community had been displaced by a rapid rush into a mode of life
that was highly complex, industrialized, scientific, and technological. From a
loose aggregation of rural households and neighborhoods, the nation, under the
impetus of technological change, became a mass society characterized by minute
structural and functional differentiation. While these rapid changes appeared to
be primarily material, the social, moral, political, economic, religious, and aesthetic aspects of life were also affected.

Change itself did not necessarily provoke crisis. Rather, crisis occurred when
individuals were unprepared to cope with and order the processes of change.
Counts believed that educational systems had failed to equip people, both cog-
nitively and attitudinally, to deal with pervasive social and cultural changes. The
crisis was further aggravated because change occurred multilaterally. That is,
alterations in one area accelerated changes and compounded crises in other areas

of life. Because of people's unwillingness to reconstruct society, turmoil and maladjustment characterized the current period of profound change.

Counts's analysis used the cultural-lag theory, which asserted that a lag occurred when human technological inventiveness outdistanced moral consciousness and social organization. An institutional crisis resulted from a whole series of maladjustments between inherited attitudes and values on the one hand, and technological innovations on the other.

One of the most serious dislocations was in the economy, where inherited values of rugged individualism impeded the establishing of a planning, cooperating, and coordinating social order. The Reconstructionist distinguished between a *planning* society and a *planned* society. In a planning society, the social design was never really completed but was continually refashioned by human creative intelligence. In contrast, a planned society, which followed a master blueprint for social change, was often locked into a predetermined mold which prevented innovative reconstruction of the plan. Thus, it was more important to use planning as a process than to arrive at a desired social destination.

To Counts, the crucial problem was to formulate a theory of education to prepare people to resolve social crises by reconstructing ideas, beliefs, and values in the light of changing conditions. In *Dare the School Build a New Social Order?* Counts challenged educators to create an educational system that recognized the emergence of a world society.[4]

U.S. education's task was twofold: (1) reconstruction of the theoretical foundations based on the U.S. cultural heritage, and (2) the experimental development of school programs that could deal with problems of acute cultural crisis and social disintegration.

Because education was always relative to a given society, U.S. education was a product of its unique heritage. For U.S. education to serve broad social needs, these needs had to be examined in terms of the cultural heritage. Then, the heritage could be reconstructed in view of social problems. In his book *The Social Foundations of Education* (1934), Counts argued that "education is always a function of time, place, and circumstances" that reflects "the hopes, fears, and aspirations of a particular time in history."[5]

Counts reasoned that a viable conception of the U.S. cultural heritage rested on two necessary conditions: (1) affirmation of the values in the democratic tradition, and (2) recognition of the dominant contemporary reality—the emergence of a technological civilization. On these two conditions, U.S. educators could create an educational theory that encouraged fundamental social reconstruction. Based on a concept of cooperative behavior in an essentially cooperative society, a synthesis of the viable elements of the democratic heritage and the requirements of science would harness scientific and technological powers for democratic purposes. The reconstruction of a comprehensive educational theory encompassed the entire range of human activities. Labor, income, property, leisure, recreation, sex, family, government, public opinion, race, ethnicity, war, peace, art, and aesthetics were appropriate to educational reconstruction.

When he challenged educators to fashion a cultural philosophy of education for modern American life, Counts was also urging them to assume the responsibilities of "educational statesmanship." Counts defined an educational statesman as a leader, a proponent of vital ways and means, a person of ideas, and an initiator of broad policy. For too long, teacher education had concentrated on mechanics and had neglected major social and economic problems. In formulating educational philosophies and programs, the educational leader was to provide national direction.

Counts's conception of the democratic ethic was uniquely associated with the U.S. experience and exalted the frontier and the popular democracy associated with Andrew Jackson, the Progressivism of Woodrow Wilson, the Liberalism of Franklin D. Roosevelt, and the attempts to create a planning society as found in the New Freedom, the New Deal, the Experimentalism of John Dewey, and the historical relativism and economic interpretations of Charles Beard.[6] In emphasizing the Progressive-Liberal strand of U.S. tradition, Counts rejected the more conservative Hamiltonianism, Social Darwinism, economic individualism, and rugged competitive capitalism. U.S. democracy was not only a political expression but was and should continue to be a product of the economic, social, moral, and aesthetic forces operating within the heritage. Democracy rested on an egalitarian social base and had to penetrate all areas of life. Inequalities of opportunity caused by wealth, race, color, or religion were subversive to the democratic ethic.

The Importance of Technology

A reconstructed program of U.S. education was directly related to a technological civilization. The application of science to the modes and techniques of life had created a new cultural force—technology—which was "the art of applying science and mechanics to the various departments of human economy." A practical and purposeful instrument, technology was marked by an emphasis on precise, orderly, and defined relationships. While its experimental character concerned the practical application of knowledge, technology was not limited to material processes and products. It was also a process, a method of solving problems and of viewing the world.

Because technology applies science to life, the role of science in a reconstructed educational philosophy should be examined. Counts saw science as humanity's most accurate instrument and method of problem solving. As a method of intelligence, science produced ordered and precise knowledge. Terming science "a method of organized and critical common sense," Counts described this method in the following manner: (1) the scientific method begins with an hypothesis growing out of previous experience, knowledge, and thought; (2) the hypothesis is tested by a process of accurate and adequate observation employing the most precise instruments; (3) data are compiled and the hypothesis proved or rejected on the basis of empirical and public verification.[7]

In commenting on science as a cultural instrument, Counts examined the characteristics of technology—the application of science to the modes and techniques of life. Technology was rational, functional, planful, dynamic, and efficient. Technological rationality rested on its freedom from tradition. Embracing immediately relevant ideas and methods that served human purposes, technology observed, inquired, and accurately and mathematically described. As quantitative reasoning tested the outcomes of technology and predicted their consequences, humanity's freedom of action increased. As it came to occupy larger areas of life, the inherent rationality of science would penetrate into society.

Because it was functional rather than purely abstract, technology was basically utilitarian. And because it was capable of being planned, technology required carefully formulated purposes, determination of directions, and conception of projected actions prior to their undertaking. The technological mode opposed impulse and caprice. The technological age required a planning and cooperating society.

Technology was dynamic. One invention or discovery initiated an ever-greater, unending cluster of new inventions. The acceleration of change initiated by inventions and discoveries was not solely material but quickly spread into the nonmaterial culture and caused subsequent economic, political, moral, and social alterations. The dynamic character of technology had accelerated social change.

Efficiency was technology's most pervasive characteristic. Technological processes achieved the greatest possible end with the least expenditure of waste and energy. Originating in the machine, the ideal of efficiency extended first to economic production and then to the entire society. Technology placed a premium on professional competence. For without the expert knowledge of the specialist, the entire productive mechanism might fall into disorder. As technology advanced, inexpert opinion yielded to trained intelligence.

Technology placed great power in human hands. Like science, it was a neutral instrument that could serve humane and enriching purposes or be an instrument of ruthless exploitation. In a nuclear age, it could be an instrument of liberation or of destruction. This powerful instrument was not a mere additive to civilization; rather, it was a system of relationships that continually altered social patterns. The technological age required continual reconstructions of the economy, society, education, government, and morality.[8]

Counts's examination of U.S. civilization affirmed two essential strains: a basic egalitarian democratic ethic, and the emergence of a scientific-industrial-technological society. These two strains were elements in a reconstructive synthesis that became the basis of his "civilizational" philosophy for U.S. education. Rather than prescribe the design of the emergent society, Counts preferred open-ended and experimental social engineering. The American people would shape their own destiny, using their own elastic democratic temperament. Counts wrote that the course of U.S. democracy depended on the ability of the people

to learn from experience, to define the problem, to formulate a program of action, to discover, appraise, and marshal the apparent and latent, the actual and potential resources of American democracy.[9]

The School and Cultural Reconstruction

In formulating a viable educational philosophy, the Reconstructionist educator gave careful attention to the school as a cultural agency. However, caution was exercised so that the school's potentiality as an instrument of reconstruction was not exaggerated. It was necessary to distinguish between education and schooling. More informal education referred to the total process of enculturation. The school as a specialized social agency was established to bring children into group life through the deliberate cultivation of socially preferred skills, knowledge, and values.

Counts believed that Americans had not sufficiently recognized the differences between education and schooling. They had identified the school with progress and regarded schooling as an unfailing solution to all problems.

However, world crises had multiplied during the period of the greatest expansion of schooling. Instead of directing social change, the school was driven aimlessly by external forces. The immature American faith in the power of schooling was based on a concept of education as a pure and independent entity isolated from social, political, and economic conflicts. This uncritical attitude inhibited the serious examination of education's moral and social foundations. Although Americans associated education solely with democracy, history demonstrated that an appropriate education existed for every society or civilization. In the twentieth century, the totalitarians proved extremely adept at using education to promote their particular ideologies. German education under the Nazis and Soviet education under the Communists demonstrated that the school could serve many masters.

Some educators, including many Progressives, erroneously believed that the school was capable of reconstructing society without the support of other social institutions. Because the school was only one of several educative social institutions, educators had to be constantly aware of the changing functions and structures of the society that determined its task. An educational theory based solely on schooling lacked reality and vitality.[10] Counts believed that the school, while important, was only one of many cultural agencies. When he asked educators to "build a new social order," Counts was urging educators to examine the culture and ally with those social forces and groups that exemplified the democratic ethic in technological use. Although educators could not reform society without the support of others, "educational statesmen" could provide leadership in building a new society. While a limited type of educational origination, it differed from the reflective theory, which held that the school should merely mirror society. Mere reflection meant that powerful pressure groups could dominate the school for their own special interests. Counts's educational theory also opposed the "four walls philosophy of the school," which asserts that educators should be concerned only with schooling and should ignore social issues.

In outlining a democratic educational program, Counts emphasized two major objectives: (1) the development of democratic habits, dispositions, and loyalties; and (2) the acquisition of knowledge and insight for intelligent participation in democratic society. Public education was to develop a feeling of competency and adequacy in the individual; an allegiance to human equality; brotherhood, dignity, and worth; loyalty to the democratic methodology of discussion, criticism, and decision; a mentality characterized by integrity and scientific spirit; and respect for talent, training, and character.[11]

Counts attacked the doctrines of educational impartiality and neutrality that demanded the teacher's complete objectivity. All education is committed to certain beliefs and values. Some criteria are necessary to guide the selection or rejection of educational goals, purposes, subjects, materials, and methods. At no point can the school assume complete neutrality and at the same time be a concrete functioning reality. For every society, there was an appropriate, distinctive education. The primary obligation of U.S. educators was to clarify the underlying assumptions and guiding principles that gave commitment and direction to the school.

As each new generation was brought into social participation, it mastered society's skills, knowledge, and attitudes. Without this transmission and perpetuation, the particular society perished. The release of human energy occurred, not by freeing individuals from tradition, but by introducing them to a vital and growing tradition.

Counts challenged both the more traditional Essentialists and Perennialists and the child-centered Progressives. Traditionalists, like the Perennialists, stressed education as purely intellectual and universal rather than involved in solving social problems. For them, the school should cultivate intellectual skills, knowledge, and habits. In the pursuit of pure knowledge, teachers were not to become involved in economic, political, and social controversies.

In addition to opposing educational traditionalism, Counts challenged child-centered Progressives. He attacked the notions of some Progressives who believed it possible to have a completely neutral school in which children were never imposed on but were totally free to develop according to their own interests. Counts held that only as social participants could children grow through their experiences. As a cultural participant, the child was imposed on by the culture and in turn made an imprint on the culture.

DEVELOPMENT THEORY AND FUTURISM

Two contemporary movements that bear a relationship to Reconstructionism are Development theory and Futurism. Development theorists and Futurists are concerned with creating a new world order.

Contemporary Development educators are concerned with bringing about worldwide change. They are especially concerned with "empowering" the economically impoverished and often politically suppressed peoples of the developing third-world nations in Asia, Africa, and Latin America. Unlike the Development theories of the 1960s that emphasized modernization from the top down by centralized government agencies, grassroots Development educators stress initiatives, planning, and implementation by people at the local level.[12]

Still another approach to using education to create a new social order comes from Futurists, educational theorists who attempt to predict the course of social and technological change and to educate for it. Their goal is not only to reduce the lag between technological change and social adaptation to it, but also to provide human beings with the knowledge and methods to control and to direct change. Futurists, such as Alvin Toffler, author of *Future Shock,* maintain that the school curriculum not only lags behind social and technological change but is also anachronistic in that it is geared to an era that has already passed.[13] While Counts argued that schools in the industrial era were still educating as if they existed in an essentially rural and agricultural society, Futurists find schools educating for the industrial rather than the postindustrial needs of the so-called information society.[14]

ISSUE-ORIENTED SCHOOLS

As noted, Social Reconstructionist educators see the schools as centers in which teachers and students grapple with society's pressing issues, not merely for academic inquiry but to engage in action-oriented research and solution. In such inquiry-oriented schools, the focus is on large social, political, economic, and educational issues. The Social Reconstructionist seeks to (1) locate schools in a social, or societal, context; (2) use schools as instruments or agencies of directed social change and reform; and (3) identify society's current social, political, economic, and educational problems. Because of their action-oriented position, the Reconstructionists encounter opposition from Perennialists, Essentialists, and even some Progressives, who fear that the schools would become politicized. These critics contend that, if applied, Social Reconstructionism would lead to the indoctrination of students for particular political purposes.

Countering the objections of their educational opponents, Social Reconstructionists contend that contemporary U.S. schools are immersed in profound social issues that daily impact their educational mission, activities, and performance. Problems such as poverty, racism, sexism, homelessness, drug abuse, and violence are social pathologies of endemic proportions in the United States. The Social Reconstructionists argue that schools cannot ignore these problems. Not only do they have an impact on society, politics, and the economy, but they also profoundly affect schools, students, and teachers. Further, these profound problems have even shaped the relationship between the school and society. For example, if students are victims of poverty, sexism, and racism, if they are hungry, and if they attend schools in a state of anxiety due to the fear of violence, then their attitudes, dispositions, and expectations about schooling will be negatively impacted. If teachers, too, feel the impact of these debilitating conditions either directly or through the lives of their students, then teaching and learning—the heart of schooling, will be affected as well. In other words, social issues outside of the school are part of the context that shape what goes on in schools.

The Social Reconstructionist's issues-oriented school is based on a belief that a definite intersection exists between the school and society. The larger society's unresolved tensions and strains have an impact on schools, teachers, and students. For Reconstructionist educators, social issues, rather than an exclusive emphasis on academic subjects and skills, constitute the underlying base of the curriculum and the educational experiences that derive from it. The school becomes a societal laboratory in which students, by engaging in action-oriented problem solving, become self empowered agents of directed social change. From such a perspective, curriculum construction is continuous rather than a process that can reach completion. Unlike the Perennialist who envisions a curriculum of eternal verities that remains unchanged in its key features, the Reconstructionist sees the curriculum as being continually reconstructed in terms of society's changing socioeconomic and political needs.

Educators who follow the Social Reconstructionist theory would see social issues problematically. For them, information about an issue is important in the research phase. However, the problem would need to be acted on and resolved by students and teachers in an active mode of learning.

In a problem-centered and action-oriented approach to major social issues, the Social Reconstructionist would ask the following focusing questions: (1) What are the viable elements in the culture and what are the areas of knowledge that explain these elements? (2) What are the problematic areas—the issues—that are impacting the society? (3) How can the problem areas be resolved so that the solutions become part of a reconstructed culture and society?

A social issue, or problem, that affects society and schooling can be analyzed in two dimensions: societally (structurally) and personally. A problem such as drug abuse may exist at the national, in some cases international, level and be found to be affecting social, political, economic, and educational institutions and infrastructures. Living in a society that exhibits major strains produces personal dissonance as well. At the local school level, drug-addicted students not only suffer the consequences of addiction but also exert a negative impact on the school, teachers, and other students. In analyzing a major social issue such as drug abuse, it becomes evident that what we consider to be a national issue, while perhaps more acute in the United States, is an international or global issue as well that affects the societies and people of other countries. While drug abuse is used as an example of a major issue, other national—and perhaps global—problems are poverty, racism, sexism, homelessness, terrorism, and violence.

Reconstructionists argue that educators—administrators and teachers alike—need to be knowledgeable about the social context in which schooling occurs. This knowledge will aid them to first understand the social situation and then to develop strategies for its reconstruction.

RECONSTRUCTIONISM'S PHILOSOPHICAL
AND IDEOLOGICAL RELATIONSHIPS

Social Reconstructionism has been influenced by Pragmatism, especially John Dewey's Experimentalism. Reconstructionists believe that by using the insights of the social sciences and the scientific method, they can create a new society. Whereas Pragmatism is open-ended, Reconstructionism tends to offer a version of the new society. Critics of the theory argue that the Reconstructionist preconceptions interfere with experimental inquiry and could lead to indoctrination in the schools.

In terms of ideology, Reconstructionists have been influenced by Liberalism, especially its modern variety, and Utopianism. Modern Liberalism, with its predilection for social reform through government regulation and intervention, is compatible with the Reconstructionist emphasis on social engineering and planning. However, the Reconstructionist proposals for a new society based on comprehensive social planning exceed the Liberal orientation to incremental reform and change.

In their desire for comprehensive social change and planning, the Reconstructionists have been influenced by the grand designs of the Utopian theorists. Although Reconstructionists have a vision of the new society, they do not regard themselves as visionaries.

Social Reconstructionists have some interesting relationships to Progressives. In fact, the socially oriented wing of the Progressive education movement was the base from which Reconstructionism emerged. George Counts and other socially oriented Progressives charged that child-centered Progressives were ignoring significant social issues and problems. For the Reconstructionists, a truly Progressive theory of education needed to examine the nature of social crisis and resolve the problems that aggravated that crisis. Child-centered Progressives countered that the Social Reconstructionists were politicizing schools and attempting to indoctrinate children according to their particular ideological creed.

Many parallels exist between Social Reconstructionism and Critical Theory, which is examined in the following chapter. Both theories agree that schools should be used to develop students' critical consciousness and ability to analyze social problems. They concur on the need to achieve a more equitable distribution of economic goods and services and to eliminate discrimination based on race, ethnicity, class, and gender. However, the historical origins of the two theories are different. Social Reconstructionism arose from the Pragmatic and Progressive temper for social, economic, and political reform. In many respects, its economic analysis was informed by Charles A. Beard's historical interpretations and George Counts's educational analyses. While economic forces certainly condition politics, society, and schooling in Reconstructionist analysis, these institutions and agencies are not completely economically determined. Although schools as institutions might be controlled by favored economic classes, schooling, even in a capitalist society, as an educational process still has liberating possibilities.

Because of its emphasis on the school as an agency of social change and social engineering, Reconstructionism is opposed by the traditional philosophies of Idealism, Realism, and Thomism, which construe education in intellectual terms. It also draws the opposition of Conservatives, Essentialists, and Perennialists, who claim that it negates the power of tradition, promotes social instability, and neglects the cultivation of essential skills and subjects. Reconstructionists, they contend, would use schools to test their social theories and turn children into sociological and pedagogical guinea pigs.

CONCLUSION

Social Reconstructionism is a theory that seeks to use the school to create a new society. A primary function of schools is to aid in the diagnosis of the crisis of modern society. Schools are to identify the major social problems that contribute to the cultural crisis and are to create the skills and attitudes that will resolve these problems. For Social Reconstructionists, teachers should not fear a committment to building a new society. Discounting charges of indoctrination, they claim that all education is a product of a particular culture. Originating with the socially oriented wing of Progressive education, Reconstructionism continues in various contemporary forms such as Development education and Futurism.

DISCUSSION QUESTIONS

1. Identify and analyze the symptoms of cultural crisis. Can and should schools seek to resolve these issues?

2. Critique Social Reconstructionism from the perspectives of Essentialism, Perennialism, and Progressivism.

3. Compare and contrast the Conservative and the Social Reconstructionist conceptions of tradition.

4. How would a Marxist critique Social Reconstructionism?

5. Indicate the ways in which Social Reconstructionism resembles ideology.

6. To what extent is Social Reconstructionism a conflict theory?

7. Examine the dynamic impact of technology on society. Use the computer, television, or the automobile as case studies.

8. Critique Counts's statement that "education is always a function of time, place, and circumstances" from the perspective of a Perennialist such as Hutchins or Adler.

9. Describe the kind of teacher that would be needed in a Reconstructionist issue-oriented school.

10. Identify the kinds of social, economic, and political problems in contemporary society that Reconstructionists would use in an issues-oriented curriculum.

INQUIRY PROJECTS

- In a paper, identify and analyze the areas of social and economic disparity and tension in the United States.
- Prepare a map that identifies areas of conflict in the world.
- Using statistics from the United Nations or the World Bank, estimate the number of people on the earth who suffer from malnutrition and extreme poverty.
- Do a content analysis of selected social studies textbooks used in secondary schools. Identify the socioeconomic problems that these books discuss. Do the authors suggest solutions to these problems?
- Review a book by George S. Counts, Theodore Brameld, William O. Stanley, or another Reconstructionist educator.
- Review a book by Alvin Toffler or another Futurist author, with special reference to education and schooling.
- Develop a unit for classroom instruction that follows the Reconstructionist approach.
- Arrange a debate on the following resolution: Resolved, the public schools will adopt a Social Reconstructionist orientation.

FURTHER READINGS

Brameld, Theodore. *Education for the Emerging Age: Newer Ends and Stronger Means.* New York: Harper & Row, 1965.

Brameld, Theodore. *Toward a Reconstructed Philosophy of Education.* New York: Holt, Rinehart and Winston, 1956.

Cernea, Michael M. *Putting People First: Sociological Variables in Rural Development.* New York: World Bank/Oxford University Press, 1985.

Coombs, Philip H. *The World Crisis in Education: The View from the Eighties.* New York: Oxford University Press, 1985.

Counts, George S. *Dare the School Build a New Social Order?* New York: John Day, 1932.

Counts, George S. *Education and American Civilization.* New York: Bureau of Publications, Teachers College, Columbia University, 1952.

Counts, George S. *Education and the Foundations of Human Freedom.* Pittsburgh: University of Pittsburgh Press, 1962.

Dennis, Lawrence. *George S. Counts and Charles A. Beard: Collaborators for Change.* Albany: State University of New York Press, 1989.

Dennis, Lawrence J., and William E. Eaton, eds. *George S. Counts: Educator for a New Age.* Carbondale: Southern Illinois University Press, 1980.

Farganis, Sondra. *Social Reconstruction of the Feminine Character.* Totowa, NJ: Rowman & Littlefield, 1986.

Gutek, Gerald L. *The Educational Theory of George S. Counts.* Columbus: Ohio State University Press, 1970.

Gutek, Gerald L. *George S. Counts and American Civilization: The Educator as Social Theorist.* Macon, GA: Mercer University Press, 1984.

Heilbroner, Robert I. *The Future as History.* New York: Harper & Row, 1968.

Honneth, Axel, ed. *Cultural-Political Interventions in the Unfinished Project of Enlightenment.* Cambridge, MA: MIT Press, 1992.

James, Michael E., ed. *Social Reconstruction Through Education: The Philoso-*

phy, History and Curricula of a Radical Ideal. Norwood, NJ: Ablex, 1995.

Miller, William C. *The Third Wave and Education's Futures.* Bloomington, IN: Phi Delta Kappa Educational Foundation, 1981.

Stanley, William B. *Curriculum for Utopia: Social Reconstructionism and Critical Pedagogy in the Postmodern Era.* Albany: State University of New York Press, 1992.

Toffler, Alvin. *Future Shock.* New York: Random House, 1970.

Toffler, Alvin, ed. *Learning for Tomorrow: The Role of the Future in Education.* New York: Random House, 1972.

ENDNOTES

1. For the history of Social Reconstructionism, see Michael E. James, *Social Reconstructionism Through Education: The Philosophy, History and Curricula of a Radical Ideal* (Norwood, NJ: Ablex, 1995).

2. Significant examples of Social Reconstructionism can be found in Theodore Brameld, *Toward a Reconstructed Philosophy of Education* (New York: Holt, Rinehart and Winston, 1956); and William O. Stanley, *Education and Social Integration* (New York: Bureau of Publications, Teachers College, Columbia University, 1953).

3. Counts's realization of the totalitarian nature of Soviet Communism can be found in George S. Counts, *The Challenge of Soviet Education* (New York: McGraw-Hill, 1957).

4. George S. Counts, *Dare the School Build a New Social Order?* (New York: John Day, 1932), pp. 17–18.

5. George S. Counts, *The Social Foundations of Education* (New York: Charles Scribner's Sons, 1934), p. 1.

6. Lawrence J. Dennis, *George S. Counts and Charles A. Beard: Collaborators for Change* (Albany: State University of New York Press, 1989).

7. George S. Counts, *Education and the Promise of America* (New York: Macmillan, 1946), pp. 87–88.

8. Counts, *Social Foundations,* pp. 70–73.

9. George S. Counts, *The Prospects of American Democracy* (New York: John Day, 1938), pp. 350–351.

10. George S. Counts, *The American Road to Culture* (New York: John Day, 1930), p. 18.

11. George S. Counts, *The Schools Can Teach Democracy* (New York: John Day, 1939), pp. 16–17.

12. Philip H. Coombs, *The World Crisis in Education: The View from the Eighties* (New York: Oxford University Press, 1985), pp. 3–31.

13. Alvin Toffler, *Future Shock* (New York: Random House, 1970), p. 353.

14. Alvin Toffler, ed., *Learning for Tomorrow: The Role of the Future in Education* (New York: Random House, 1974); also see William C. Miller, *The Third Wave and Education's Futures* (Bloomington, IN: Phi Delta Kappa Educational Foundation, 1981).

Chapter 5

William James

1892–1893	Travels to Europe.
1897	Publishes *The Will to Believe and Other Essays on Popular Psychology*.
1899	Publishes *Talks to Teachers*.
1899–1902	Travels to Europe to try to regain his health.
1901–1902	Gives Gifford Lectures, published as *The Varieties of Religious Experience*.
1906	Gives the Lowell Institute Lectures, published as *Pragmatism*.
1907	Retires from Harvard.
1908	Presents papers at the Hibbert Lectures at Manchester College, Oxford, published as *A Pluralistic Universe*.
1910	Dies August 26, at Chocorua, New Hampshire.
1912	*Essays in Radical Empiricism* are published.

Introduction

In his introduction to *The Writings of William James: A Comprehensive Edition,* John McDermott reminds the reader of Julius Seelye Bixler's famous warning against excerpting James: "The isolated reference from James is always unreliable." It is easy, far too easy, to take James's own words, wrest them from their context and turn James into a raving, easily duped mystic or into a narrow-minded entrepreneur who equated truth with utility. James was interested in the varieties of religious experience, including extrasensory perception, and he was concerned with what he called the "cash value" of an idea, but a careful reading of his work will show that his thinking is far richer, far more complex than the labels mentioned above suggest.

William James was born into a family that prized and produced genius. It is hard to imagine a more famous nineteenth-century family than the Jameses. The father, Henry Sr., was perhaps the preeminent theologian of his day. Henry Jr., with his wonderfully elaborate sentences and his disdain for things American, became the embodiment of the expatriate novelist, finding aesthetic salvation in England and on the Continent. In addition, recent biographies—and no American family this side of the Kennedys has been subject to as many biographical accounts as the James clan—suggest that in this family of geniuses, the most powerful may have been also the most fragile: Had Alice James received the same support as her more fortunate brothers, there is reason to believe that her intellectual star would now shine as brightly as her brothers' or her father's.

Of the three major American pragmatists—Charles Sanders Peirce, William James, and John Dewey—James's reputation has suffered the deepest and most significant shifts. Peirce (1839–1914), as the philosopher most concerned with the logic of pragmatism and with its theoretical underpinnings, has always been esteemed by the philosophical community. Dewey's reputation has ebbed and flowed, but his work has always been in print, and even when his reputation was at its lowest, he was always considered a philosopher, although his detractors would attach "muddle-headed" to the noun. William James, however, is quite another story. During his glory days at Harvard (1876–1907) no philosopher was held in higher esteem. The publication of his most technical work, *The Principles of Psychology,* was one of the major events of intellectual history of the nineteenth century. While it may not have had the dramatic impact on popular life that Darwin's *Origin of Species* had, it certainly helped revolutionize thinking in psychology and philosophy. After his death, however, James's reputation suffered a decline. His books went out of print, and academicians, when they could refrain from snickering at him, treated him as hopelessly naive, lacking all philosophical rigor, and unrelentingly eccentric. Recently, in large part due to John McDermott's masterful collection of James's work but also due to changes in philosophy itself—changes including the entrance of minorities into the profession of philosophy and the expansion of philosophy into applied areas such as education and environmental issues—James's reputation has been restored. History suggests it would be foolhardy to think that further shifts will not occur.

Part of the difficulty with James, one of the reasons that his reputation has suffered such violent change, is that James presented his work in two distinct forms. His theoretical work, especially as it appears in *Principles of Psychology* and *Essays in Radical Empiricism,* has the tightness and rigor one would normally expect from a philosophical document. Unfortunately, the writing is frequently inaccessible to educators who have an interest in the philosophical dimensions of education. Simply, the bridge from philosophical theory to educational practice is not apparent. Thus James's technical work tends to get ignored.

On the other hand, much of James's nontechnical writing is comprised of speeches that he gave to popular audiences—teachers, ministers, and so on. They are frequently pithy and invariably evocative, but it is a stretch to suggest that they are rigorous. They read exactly as what they are—chatty speeches about matters of popular interest.

The difficulty, then, is how to present James so that the reader can see his educational importance. To solve this difficulty, we, as editors, will be a bit more prescriptive than we have been in previous sections and urge the reader to keep in mind, when reading James, two basic points: (1) James's world, the world of the pragmatists in general, is unfinished and open. It is a world both precarious and stable—a world in which we can predict, frequently accurately, but a world that, at crucial moments, tends to slip outside our theories and preconceived notions. (2) In order to make one's way in this world, in order to achieve one's end, one must be sensitive to the varieties of experience. The educated person must listen and look hard: She or he must look at things, even the most mundane things, with a "'fresh eye," with the eye of a poet or an artist. This sensitivity to experience, this willingness to look and listen hard is at the very heart of James's educational theory and is constitutive of the educated person.

The following excerpts are all taken from what is considered to be James's popular writing. Embrace, if you will, the two points, remember Bixler's remark about

Jamesian excerpts, and mentally "complete" James' popular thought with its technical foundation. Finally, James' "What Pragmatism Means" might serve as a prism through which the careful reader can examine the works of later pragmatists such as John Dewey, Cornel West, and Richard Rorty.

From *Talks to Teachers* (1899)

"On a Certain Blindness in Human Beings"

Our judgments concerning the worth of things, big or little, depend on the *feelings* the things arouse in us. Where we judge a thing to be precious in consequence of the *idea* we frame of it, this is only because the idea is itself associated already with a feeling. If we were radically feelingless, and if ideas were the only things our mind could entertain, we should lose all our likes and dislikes at a stroke, and be unable to point to any one situation or experience in life more valuable or significant than any other.

Now the blindness in human beings, of which this discourse will treat, is the blindness with which we all are afflicted in regard to the feelings of creatures and people different from ourselves.

We are practical beings, each of us with limited functions and duties to perform. Each is bound to feel intensely the importance of his own duties and the significance of the situations that call these forth. But this feeling is in each of us a vital secret, for sympathy with which we vainly look to others. The others are too much absorbed in their own vital secrets to take an interest in ours. Hence the stupidity and injustice of our opinions, so far as they deal with the significance of alien lives. Hence the falsity of our judgments, so far as they presume to decide in an absolute way on the value of other persons' conditions or ideals.

Take our dogs and ourselves, connected as we are by a tie more intimate than most ties in this world; and yet, outside of that tie of friendly fondness, how insensible, each of us, to all that makes life significant for the other!—we to the rapture of bones under hedges, or smells of trees and lamp-posts, they to the delights of literature and art. As you sit reading the most moving romance you ever fell upon, what sort of a judge is your fox-terrier of your behavior? With all his good will toward you, the nature of your conduct is absolutely excluded from his comprehension. To sit there like a senseless statue, when you might be taking him to walk and throwing sticks for him to catch! What queer disease is this that comes over you every day, of holding things and staring at them like that for hours together, paralyzed of motion and vacant of all conscious life? The African savages came nearer the truth; but they, too, missed it, when they gathered wonderingly round one of our American travellers who, in the interior, had

From *The Writings of William James*, edited by John J. McDermott © 1977 University of Chicago Press, pp. 629–635.

just come into possession of a stray copy of the New York *Commercial Advertiser*, and was devouring it column by column. When he got through, they offered him a high price for the mysterious object; and, being asked for what they wanted it, they said: "For an eye medicine,"—that being the only reason they could conceive of for the protracted bath which he had given his eyes upon its surface.

The spectator's judgment is sure to miss the root of the matter, and to possess no truth. The subject judged knows a part of the world of reality which the judging spectator fails to see, knows more while the spectator knows less; and, whenever there is conflict of opinion and difference of vision, we are bound to believe that the truer side is the side that feels the more, and not the side that feels the less.

Let me take a personal example of the kind that befalls each one of us daily:—

Some years ago, while journeying in the mountains of North Carolina, I passed by a large number of "coves," as they call them there, or heads of small valleys between the hills, which had been newly cleared and planted. The impression on my mind was one of unmitigated squalor. The settler had in every case cut down the more manageable trees, and left their charred stumps standing. The larger trees he had girdled and killed, in order that their foliage should not cast a shade. He had then built a log cabin, plastering its chinks with clay, and had set up a tall zigzag rail fence around the scene of his havoc, to keep the pigs and cattle out. Finally, he had irregularly planted the intervals between the stumps and trees with Indian corn, which grew among the chips; and there he dwelt with his wife and babes—an axe, a gun, a few utensils, and some pigs and chickens feeding in the woods, being the sum total of his possessions.

The forest had been destroyed; and what had "improved" it out of existence was hideous, a sort of ulcer, without a single element of artificial grace to make up for the loss of Nature's beauty. Ugly, indeed, seemed the life of the squatter, scudding, as the sailors say, under bare poles, beginning again away back where our first ancestors started, and by hardly a single item the better off for all the achievements of the intervening generations.

Talk about going back to nature! I said to myself, oppressed by the dreariness, as I drove by. Talk of a country life for one's old age and for one's children! Never thus, with nothing but the bare ground and one's bare hands to fight the battle! Never, without the best spoils of culture woven in! The beauties and commodities gained by the centuries are sacred. They are our heritage and birthright. No modern person ought to be willing to live a day in such a state of rudimentariness and denudation.

Then I said to the mountaineer who was driving me, "What sort of people are they who have to make these new clearings?" "All of us," he replied. "Why, we ain't happy here, unless we are getting one of these coves under cultivation." I instantly felt that I had been losing the whole inward significance of the situation. Because to me the clearings spoke of naught but denudation, I thought that to those whose sturdy arms and obedient axes had made them they could tell no other story. But, when *they* looked on the hideous stumps, what they thought of was personal victory. The chips, the girdled trees, and the vile split rails spoke of honest sweat, persistent toil and final reward. The cabin was a warrant of safety for self and wife and babes. In short, the clearing, which to me was a mere ugly picture on the retina, was to them a symbol redolent with moral memories and sang a very pæan of duty, struggle, and success.

I had been as blind to the peculiar ideality of their conditions as they certainly would also have been to the ideality of mine, had they had a peep at my strange indoor academic ways of life at Cambridge.

Wherever a process of life communicates an eagerness to him who lives it, there the life becomes genuinely significant. Sometimes the eagerness is more knit up with the motor activities, sometimes with the perceptions, sometimes with the imagination, sometimes with reflective thought. But, wherever it is found, there is the zest, the tingle, the excitement of reality; and there *is* "importance" in the only real and positive sense in which importance ever anywhere can be.

Robert Louis Stevenson has illustrated this by a case, drawn from the sphere of the imagination, in an essay which I really think deserves to become immortal, both for the truth of its matter and the excellence of its form.

"Toward the end of September," Stevenson writes, "when school-time was drawing near, and the nights were already black, we would begin to sally from our respective villas, each equipped with a tin bull's-eye lantern. The thing was so well known that it had worn a rut in the commerce of Great Britain; and the grocers, about the due time, began to garnish their windows with our particular brand of luminary. We wore them buckled to the waist upon a cricket belt, and over them, such was the rigor of the game, a buttoned top-coat. They smelled noisomely of blistered tin. They never burned aright, though they would always burn our fingers. Their use was naught, the pleasure of them merely fanciful, and yet a boy with a bull's-eye under his top-coat asked for nothing more. The fishermen used lanterns about their boats, and it was from them, I suppose, that we had got the hint; but theirs were not bull's-eyes, nor did we ever play at being fishermen. The police carried them at their belts, and we had plainly copied them in that; yet we did not pretend to be policemen. Burglars, indeed, we may have had some haunting thought of; and we had certainly an eye to past ages when lanterns were more common, and to certain story-books in which we had found them to figure very largely. But take it for all in all, the pleasure of the thing was substantive; and to be a boy with a bull's-eye under his top-coat was good enough for us.

"When two of these asses met, there would be an anxious 'Have you got your lantern?' and a gratified 'Yes!' That was the shibboleth, and very needful, too; for, as it was the rule to keep our glory contained, none could recognize a lantern-bearer unless (like the polecat) by the smell. Four or five would sometimes climb into the belly of a ten-man lugger, with nothing but the thwarts above them,—for the cabin was usually locked,—or chose out some hollow of the links where the wind might whistle overhead. Then the coats would be unbuttoned, and the bull's-eyes discovered; and in the chequering glimmer, under the huge, windy hall of the night, and cheered by a rich steam of toasting tinware, these fortunate young gentlemen would crouch together in the cold sand of the links, or on the scaly bilges of the fishing-boat, and delight them with inappropriate talk. Woe is me that I cannot give some specimens! . . . But the talk was but a condiment, and these gatherings themselves only accidents in the career of the lantern-bearer. The essence of this bliss was to walk by yourself in the black night, the slide shut, the top-coat buttoned, not a ray escaping, whether to conduct your footsteps or to make your glory public,—a mere pillar of darkness in the dark; and all the while, deep down in the privacy of your fool's heart, to know you had a bull's-eye at your belt, and to exult and sing over the knowledge.

"It is said that a poet has died young in the breast of the most stolid. It may be contended rather that a (somewhat minor) bard in almost every case survives, and is the spice of life to his possessor. Justice is not done to the versatility and the unplumbed childishness of man's imagination. His life from without may seem but a rude mound of mud: there will be some golden chamber at the heart of it, in which he dwells delighted; and for as dark as his pathway seems to the observer, he will have some kind of bull's-eye at his belt. . . .

"There is one fable that touches very near the quick of life,—the fable of the monk who passed into the woods, heard a bird break into song, hearkened for a trill or two, and found himself at his return a stranger at his convent gates; for he had been absent fifty years, and of all his comrades there survived but one to recognize him. It is not only in the woods that this enchanter carols, though perhaps he is native there. He sings in the most doleful places. The miser hears him and chuckles, and his days are moments. With no more apparatus than an evil-smelling lantern, I have evoked him on the naked links. All life that is not merely mechanical is spun out of two strands,—seeking for that bird and hearing him. And it is just this that makes life so hard to value, and the delight of each so incommunicable. And it is just a knowledge of this, and a remembrance of those fortunate hours in which the bird *has* sung to *us*, that fills us with such wonder when we turn to the pages of the realist. There, to be sure, we find a picture of life in so far as it consists of mud and of old iron, cheap desires and cheap fears, that which we are ashamed to remember and that which we are careless whether we forget; but of the note of that time-devouring nightingale we hear no news. . . .

"Say that we came [in such a realistic romance] on some such business as that of my lantern-bearers on the links, and described the boys as very cold, spat upon by flurries of rain, and drearily surrounded, all of which they were; and their talk as silly and indecent, which it certainly was. To the eye of the observer they *are* wet and cold and drearily surrounded; but ask themselves, and they are in the heaven of a recondite pleasure, the ground of which is an ill-smelling lantern.

"For, to repeat, the ground of a man's joy is often hard to hit. It may hinge at times upon a mere accessory, like the lantern; it may reside in the mysterious inwards of psychology. . . . It has so little bond with externals . . . that it may even touch them not, and the man's true life, for which he consents to live, lie together in the field of fancy. . . . In such a case the poetry runs underground. The observer (poor soul, with his documents!) is all abroad. For to look at the man is but to count deception. We shall see the trunk from which he draws his nourishment; but he himself is above and abroad in the green dome of foliage, hummed through by winds and nested in by nightingales. And the true realism were that of the poets, to climb after him like a squirrel, and catch some glimpse of the heaven in which he lives. And the true realism, always and everywhere, is that of the poets: to find out where joy resides, and give it a voice far beyond singing.

"For to miss the joy is to miss all. In the joy of the actors lies the sense of any action. That is the explanation, that the excuse. To one who has not the secret of the lanterns the scene upon the links is meaningless. And hence the haunting and truly spectral unreality of realistic books. . . . In each we miss the personal poetry, the enchanted atmosphere, that rainbow work of fancy that clothes what is naked and seems to ennoble what is base; in each, life falls dead like dough, instead of soaring away like a balloon into the colors of the sunset; each is true, each inconceivable; for no man lives in the external truth among salts and acids, but in the warm, phantasmagoric chamber of his brain, with the painted windows and the storied wall."[1]

These paragraphs are the best thing I know in all Stevenson. "To miss the joy is to miss all." Indeed, it is. Yet we are but finite, and each one of us has some single specialized vocation of his own. And it seems as if energy in the service of its particular duties might be got only by hardening the heart toward everything unlike them. Our deadness toward all but one particular kind of joy would thus be the price we inevitably have to pay for being practical creatures. Only in some pitiful dreamer, some philosopher, poet, or romancer, or when the common practical man becomes a lover, does the hard externality give way, and a gleam of insight into the ejective world, as Clifford called it, the vast world of inner life beyond us, so different from that of outer seeming, illuminate our mind. Then the whole scheme of our customary values gets confounded, then our self is riven and its narrow interests fly to pieces, then a new centre and a new perspective must be found.

The change is well described by my colleague, Josiah Royce:—

"What, then, is our neighbor? Thou hast regarded his thought, his feeling, as somehow different from thine. Thou hast said, 'A pain in him is not like a pain in me, but something far easier to bear.' He seems to thee a little less living than thou; his life is dim, it is cold, it is a pale fire beside thy own burning desires. . . . So, dimly and by instinct hast thou lived with thy neighbor, and hast known him not, being blind. Thou hast made [of him] a thing, no Self at all. Have done with this illusion, and simply try to learn the truth. Pain is pain, joy is joy, everywhere, even as in thee. In all the songs of the forest birds; in all the cries of the wounded and dying, struggling in the captor's power; in the boundless sea where the myriads of water-creatures strive and die; amid all the countless hordes of savage men; in all sickness and sorrow; in all exultation and hope, everywhere, from the lowest to the noblest, the same conscious, burning, wilful life is found, endlessly manifold as the forms of the living creatures, unquenchable as the fires of the sun, real as these impulses that even now throb in thine

---

[1] "The Lantern-bearers," in the volume entitled *Across the Plains*. Abridged in the quotation.

own little selfish heart. Lift up thy eyes, behold that life, and then turn away, and forget it as thou canst; but, if thou hast *known* that, thou hast begun to know thy duty."[2]

From *Pragmatism* (1906)

"What Pragmatism Means"

Some years ago, being with a camping party in the mountains, I returned from a solitary ramble to find every one engaged in a ferocious metaphysical dispute. The *corpus* of the dispute was a squirrel—a live squirrel supposed to be clinging to one side of a tree-trunk; while over against the tree's opposite side a human being was imagined to stand. This human witness tries to get sight of the squirrel by moving rapidly round the tree, but no matter how fast he goes, the squirrel moves as fast in the opposite direction, and always keeps the tree between himself and the man, so that never a glimpse of him is caught. The resultant metaphysical problem now is this: *Does the man go round the squirrel or not?* He goes round the tree, sure enough, and the squirrel is on the tree; but does he go round the squirrel? In the unlimited leisure of the wilderness, discussion had been worn threadbare. Everyone had taken sides, and was obstinate; and the numbers on both sides were even. Each side, when I appeared, therefore appealed to me to make it a majority. Mindful of the scholastic adage that whenever you meet a contradiction you must make a distinction, I immediately sought and found one, as follows: "Which party is right," I said," depends on what you *practically mean* by 'going round' the squirrel. If you mean passing from the north of him to the east, then to the south, then to the west, and then to the north of him again, obviously the man does go round him, for he occupies these successive positions. But if on the contrary you mean being first in front of him, then on the right of him, then behind him, then on his left, and finally in front again, it is quite as obvious that the man fails to go round him, for by the compensating movements the squirrel makes, he keeps his belly turned towards the man all the time, and his back turned away. Make the distinction, and there is no occasion for any farther dispute. You are both right and both wrong according as you conceive the verb 'to go round' in one practical fashion or the other."

Although one or two of the hotter disputants called my speech a shuffling evasion, saying they wanted no quibbling or scholastic hair-splitting, but meant just plain honest English "round," the majority seemed to think that the distinction had assuaged the dispute.

I tell this trivial anecdote because it is a peculiarly simple example of what I wish now to speak of as *the pragmatic method.* The pragmatic method is primarily a method of settling metaphysical disputes that otherwise might be interminable. Is the world one or many?—fated or free?—material or spiritual?—here are

---

[2] *The Religious Aspect of Philosophy,* pp. 157–162 (abridged).

From *The Writings of William James,* edited by John J. McDermott, © 1977 University of Chicago Press, pp. 376–380.

notions either of which may or may not hold good of the world; and disputes over such notions are unending. The pragmatic method in such cases is to try to interpret each notion by tracing its respective practical consequences. What difference would it practically make to any one if this notion rather than that notion were true? If no practical difference whatever can be traced, then the alternatives mean practically the same thing, and all dispute is idle. Whenever a dispute is serious, we ought to be able to show some practical difference that must follow from one side or the other's being right.

A glance at the history of the idea will show you still better what pragmatism means. The term is derived from the same Greek word πραγμα, meaning action, from which our words "practice" and "practical" come. It was first introduced into philosophy by Mr. Charles Peirce in 1878. In an article entitled "How to Make Our Ideas Clear," in the *Popular Science Monthly* for January of that year[1] Mr. Peirce, after pointing out that our beliefs are really rules for action, said that, to develop a thought's meaning, we need only determine what conduct it is fitted to produce: that conduct is for us its sole significance. And the tangible fact at the root of all our thought-distinctions, however subtle, is that there is no one of them so fine as to consist in anything but a possible difference of practice. To attain perfect clearness in our thoughts of an object, then, we need only consider what conceivable effects of a practical kind the object may involve—what sensations we are to expect from it, and what reactions we must prepare. Our conception of these effects, whether immediate or remote, is then for us the whole of our conception of the object, so far as that conception has positive significance at all.

This is the principle of Peirce, the principle of pragmatism. It lay entirely unnoticed by any one for twenty years, until I, in an address before Professor Howison's philosophical union at the University of California, brought it forward again and made a special application of it to religion. By that date (1898) the times seemed ripe for its reception. The word "pragmatism" spread, and at present it fairly spots the pages of the philosophic journals. On all hands we find the "pragmatic movement" spoken of, sometimes with respect, sometimes with contumely, seldom with clear understanding. It is evident that the term applies itself conveniently to a number of tendencies that hitherto have lacked a collective name, and that it has "come to stay."

To take in the importance of Peirce's principle, one must get accustomed to applying it to concrete cases. I found a few years ago that Ostwald, the illustrious Leipzig chemist, had been making perfectly distinct use of the principle of pragmatism in his lectures on the philosophy of science, though he had not called it by that name.

"All realities influence our practice," he wrote me, "and that influence is their meaning for us. I am accustomed to put questions to my classes in this way: In what respects would the world be different if this alternative or that

---

[1] Translated in the *Revue Philosophique* for January, 1879 (vol. vii).

were true? If I can find nothing that would become different, then the alternative has no sense."

That is, the rival views mean practically the same thing, and meaning, other than practical, there is for us none. Ostwald in a published lecture gives this example of what he means. Chemists have long wrangled over the inner constitution of certain bodies called "tautomerous." Their properties seemed equally consistent with the notion that an instable hydrogen atom oscillates inside of them, or that they are instable mixtures of two bodies. Controversy raged, but never was decided. "It would never have begun," says Ostwald, "if the combatants had asked themselves what particular experimental fact could have been made different by one or the other view being correct. For it would then have appeared that no difference of fact could possibly ensue; and the quarrel was as unreal as if, theorizing in primitive times about the raising of dough by yeast, one party should have invoked a 'brownie,' while another insisted on an 'elf' as the true cause of the phenomenon."[2]

It is astonishing to see how many philosophical disputes collapse into insignificance the moment you subject them to this simple test of tracing a concrete consequence. There can *be* no difference anywhere that doesn't *make* a difference elsewhere—no difference in abstract truth that doesn't express itself in a difference in concrete fact and in conduct consequent upon that fact, imposed on somebody, somehow, somewhere, and somewhen. The whole function of philosophy ought to be to find out what definite difference it will make to you and me, at definite instants of our life, if this world-formula or that world-formula be the true one.

There is absolutely nothing new in the pragmatic method. Socrates was an adept at it. Aristotle used it methodically. Locke, Berkeley, and Hume made momentous contributions to truth by its means. Shadworth Hodgson keeps insisting that realities are only what they are "known as." But these forerunners of pragmatism used it in fragments: they were preluders only. Not until in our time has it generalized itself, become conscious of a universal mission, pretended to a conquering destiny. I believe in that destiny, and I hope I may end by inspiring you with my belief.

Pragmatism represents a perfectly familiar attitude in philosophy, the empiricist attitude, but it represents it, as it seems to me, both in a more radical and in a less objectionable form than it has ever yet assumed. A pragmatist turns his back resolutely and once for all upon a lot of inveterate habits dear to professional philosophers. He turns away from abstraction and insufficiency, from verbal solutions, from bad *a priori* reasons, from fixed principles, closed systems, and pretended absolutes and origins. He turns towards concreteness

---

[2] "Theorie und Praxis," *Zeitsch. des Oesterreichischen Ingenieur u. Architecten-Vereines,* 1905, Nr. 4 u. 6. I find a still more radical pragmatism than Ostwald's in an address by Professor W. S. Franklin: "I think that the sickliest notion of physics, even if a student gets it, is that it is 'the science of masses, molecules, and the ether.' And I think that the healthiest notion, even if a student does not wholly get it, is that physics is the science of the ways of taking hold of bodies and pushing them!" (*Science,* January 2, 1903.)

and adequacy, towards facts, towards action and towards power. That means the empiricist temper regnant and the rationalist temper sincerely given up. It means the open air and possibilities of nature, as against dogma, artificiality, and the pretense of finality in truth.

At the same time it does not stand for any special results. It is a method only. But the general triumph of that method would mean an enormous change in what I called in my last lecture the "temperament" of philosophy. Teachers of the ultra-rationalistic type would be frozen out, much as the courtier type is frozen out in republics, as the ultra-montane type of priest is frozen out in protestant lands. Science and metaphysics would come much nearer together, would in fact work absolutely hand in hand.

Metaphysics has usually followed a very primitive kind of quest. You know how men have always hankered after unlawful magic, and you know what a great part in magic *words* have always played. If you have his name, or the formula of incantation that binds him, you can control the spirit, genie, afrite, or whatever the power may be. Solomon knew the names of all the spirits and having their names, he held them subject to his will. So the universe has always appeared to the natural mind as a kind of enigma, of which the key must be sought in the shape of some illuminating or power-bringing word or name. That word names the universe's *principle*, and to possess it is after a fashion to possess the universe itself. "God," "Matter," "Reason," "the Absolute," "Energy," are so many solving names. You can rest when you have them. You are at the end of your metaphysical quest.

But if you follow the pragmatic method, you cannot look on any such word as closing your quest. You must bring out of each word its practical cash-value, set it at work within the stream of your experience. It appears less as a solution, then, than as a program for more work, and more particularly as an indication of the ways in which existing realities may be *changed*.

Theories thus become instruments, not answers to enigmas, in which we can rest. We don't lie back upon them, we move forward, and, on occasion, make nature over again by their aid. Pragmatism unstiffens all our theories, limbers them up and sets each one at work. Being nothing essentially new, it harmonizes with many ancient philosophic tendencies. It agrees with nominalism for instance, in always appealing to particulars; with utilitarianism in emphasizing practical aspects; with positivism in its disdain for verbal solutions, useless questions and metaphysical abstractions.

All these, you see, are *anti-intellectualist* tendencies. Against rationalism as a pretension and a method pragmatism is fully armed and militant. But, at the outset, at least, it stands for no particular results. It has no dogmas, and no doctrines save its method. As the young Italian pragmatist Papini has well said, it lies in the midst of our theories, like a corridor in a hotel. Innumerable chambers open out of it. In one you may find a man writing an atheistic volume; in the next some one on his knees praying for faith and strength; in a third a chemist investigating a body's properties. In a fourth a system of idealistic metaphysics is being excogitated; in a fifth the impossibility of metaphysics is being shown.

But they all own the corridor, and all must pass through it if they want a practicable way of getting into or out of their respective rooms.

No particular results then, so far, but only an attitude of orientation, is what the pragmatic method means. *The attitude of looking away from first things, principles, "categories," supposed necessities: and of looking towards last things, fruits, consequences, facts.*

Questions

1. What is the blindness to which William James alludes?
2. What is the difference between the spectator's judgment and the subject's judgment?
3. James suggests that merely mechanical actions are meaningless. Do you agree? Explain.
4. How would you structure things in a classroom so that they would not be merely mechanical?
5. What does pragmatism mean?
6. Is James's view of reality consistent with the view implicit in the discipline of science as you have experienced it in school? Explain.
7. What, for James, is a theory?
8. Do you agree with James's understanding of theory? Explain.
9. What is Peirce's principle?
10. Why is pragmatism such a radical empiricism?

Chapter 6

John Dewey

TIME LINE FOR DEWEY

1859	Is born October 20 in Burlington, Vermont.
1875	Enters the University of Vermont.
1879	Receives Bachelor's degree.
1879–1881	Teaches high school at Oil City, Pennsylvania.
1881	Studies philosophy with H. A. P. Torrey at Johns Hopkins University.
1882	Enters graduate school.
1884	Receives Ph.D. from Johns Hopkins.
1884–1894	Teaches philosophy at the University of Michigan.
1886	Marries Alice Chipman.
1894	Is appointed chairman of the Department of Philosophy, Psychology, and Pedagogy at the University of Chicago.
	Starts Lab School at University of Chicago.
1895	Suffers loss of son, Morris, from diphtheria while in Milan. The Deweys later return to Italy and adopt an orphan boy, Sabino.
1897	Publishes "My Pedagogic Creed."
1900	Publishes *The School and Society*.
1902	Publishes *The Child and the Curriculum*.
1904	Is appointed professor of philosophy at Columbia University.

1904	Suffers the loss of son, Gordon, from typhoid fever while vacationing in Ireland.
1910	Publishes *How We Think.*
1915	Establishes and is the first president of the American Association of University Professors.
1916	Publishes *Democracy and Education.*
1919–1928	Gives lectures in Japan, China, Turkey, Mexico, and Russia.
1920	Publishes *Reconstruction of Philosophy,* based on lectures given at the Imperial University, Japan.
1922	Publishes *Human Nature and Conduct.*
1925	Publishes *Experience and Nature.*
1927	Suffers loss of his wife, Alice.
1930	Is named professor emeritus at Columbia University.
1934	Publishes *Art as Experience* and *A Common Faith.*
1937	Serves as chairman of the commission of inquiry into the charges made against Leon Trotsky (Mexico City).
1938	Publishes *Experience and Education.*
1939	Publishes *Freedom and Culture.*
1946	Marries Roberta Lowitz Grant. They adopt two children. Publishes *Problems of Men.*
1949	Publishes, with Arthur Bentley, *Knowing and the Known.*
1952	Dies June 1 in New York City.

Introduction

Born in 1859—the same year that Horace Mann died and that saw the publication of Charles Darwin's *Origin of Species*—Dewey lived through the Civil War, two world wars, the Great Depression, and numerous lesser conflicts, and died as the cold war emerged full blown on the global scene. During his lifetime, the United States was transformed from a largely agrarian, experimental republic into the major industrial and military power in the world. Growing up in Puritan New England, Dewey would gradually abandon his religious foundations, moving, as he explains, "from absolutism to experimentalism." Attaining his undergraduate degree from the University of Vermont and eventually his Ph.D. from Johns Hopkins University, Dewey retained his religious commitment through his professorship at the University of Michigan in the 1880s and 1890s. As a young man, Dewey embraced the Social Gospel movement in hopes of connecting his commitment to democracy to an absolutist metaphysics—Hegelian idealism.

His commitment to social justice and democratic principles never waned, but by the early 1890s, Dewey had begun to distance himself from otherworldly metaphysics. Upon moving to Chicago in 1894 to chair the Department of Philosophy, Psychology, and Pedagogy at the University of Chicago, Dewey stopped participating in religious activities. By this time he had transformed his metaphysical idealism into pragmatic naturalism. Finally, feeling comfortable that his commitment to democratic principles could be sustained by grounding them in experience, Dewey spent much of the remainder of his life working out the implications of this philosophical shift for his social, political, and educational ideas.

The years Dewey lived in Chicago were productive ones. Here he continued his commitment to social justice by working with Jane Addams at Hull House, experiencing firsthand the dehumanizing effects that America's transformation into an industrialized and urbanized oligarchy produced. Here, too, Dewey established his famous Lab School, a living, self-correcting community, as a testing ground for his evolving educational ideas. Here, too, he emerged, along with William James and Charles S. Peirce, as a founder of that uniquely American brand of philosophy known as pragmatism.

Leaving Chicago in 1904, Dewey assumed a professorship of philosophy at Columbia University in New York City, a position he held until his retirement in 1929. In addition to teaching, writing, and numerous other academic responsibilities, Dewey struggled to find ways to construct "the Great Community" and to make the world "safe for democracy." Initially supportive of Wilson's war policy—for which his former student, Randolph Bourne, criticized him for falling "prey to the very mistakes his philosophy was designed to prevent"[1]—Dewey participated in the quixotic Outlaw War movement during the postwar period. During these years and throughout his life, "Dewey was the most important advocate of participatory democracy, that is of the belief that democracy as an ethical ideal calls upon men and women to build communities in which the necessary opportunities and resources are available for every individual to fully realize his or her particular capacities and powers through participation in political, social, and cultural life."[2]

Though officially retired, Dewey remained remarkably active during the last 23 years of his life. He continued his prolific writing, publishing major works on aesthetics, religion, politics, education, logic, and epistemology. He remained active in social causes, including traveling to Mexico to chair the commission of inquiry investigating the charges leveled against Leon Trotsky. Maintaining an active lifestyle until his death in 1952, Dewey married in 1946 a woman almost half his age and with her adopted two Belgian war orphans.[3]

As suggested earlier, Dewey was a prolific scholar throughout his life; he published scores of books and pamphlets, hundreds of articles for scholarly and popular journals and magazines, and gave innumerable speeches and lectures—public as well as academic—on topics ranging from Hegelian metaphysics to woman's suffrage. Indeed, it is not an exaggeration to suggest that from 1900 to 1940, Dewey published more each year than many small college faculties produced during all of these years. Unfortunately, Dewey did not always write well. As Justice Oliver Wendell Holmes charges: "Dewey writes as the creator would write, if he were intent on explaining all of his creation but was hopelessly inarticulate." Dewey's works are often misunderstood, but more frequently Dewey is not read. As John

Novak explains, "John Dewey is like the Bible—often alluded to (both by his supporters and detractors) but seldom read. . . ."[4]

Students who might be interested in Dewey's work, and who clearly could benefit from it, are often overwhelmed by the sheer volume of it. Those ambitious enough to dive into one of Dewey's works are likely to find his prose stiff and lacking in imagination. In addition, while there is an abundance of literature about Dewey, much of it treats him either as a saint or a villain. In this secondary literature, most of it published during this century, Dewey has been reviled and praised, criticized and attacked for being the father of progressive education, a communist dupe and a hopeless anticommunist, a pacifist and a turncoat to pacifist ideals, a secular humanist, and the founder of all things good (and bad) in American education.

A work like this one can do little to answer all the questions about Dewey and his influence on education other than to suggest that Dewey was a highly complex thinker whose thought could never be captured by any reductionist label. What this work can do—by introducing the reader to carefully selected excerpts from Dewey's works—is whet the reader's appetite for more information about this remarkable figure in American educational thought. If this work is successful, you will be motivated to further investigate both the man and his thought by reading Dewey's autobiographical essay "From Absolutism to Experimentalism"; George Dykhuizen's *The Life and Mind of John Dewey,* a work already quoted in this brief introduction; Robert B. Westbrook's recently published *John Dewey and American Democracy;* as well as the many seminal works Dewey published during his long and distinguished life.

Here we will focus on three works of John Dewey: "My Pedagogic Creed," published in 1897; an excerpt from *Democracy and Education* (1916), which for most of his career Dewey claimed to be the work in which his philosophy was best developed; and an excerpt from *Experience and Education* (1938), which might be read as a corrective to Dewey's followers in the progressive education movement.

"My Pedagogic Creed" is, in many way, Dewey's gift to scholars. Over the course of a few pages he tells what he believes about education, the school, subject matter, the nature of method, and the relation of the school to social progress. Dewey writes of the psychological and sociological sides of education, the child's cultural inheritance, discipline and interest, the relationship of the school to the neighborhood, activity and images in teaching, the connection between immediate experience and traditional school subject matters and disciplines, and finally the school as an instrument of social progress and the teacher as the "harbinger" of a new social order. In the middle of all that, Dewey defines education as "a continual process of reconstruction of experience." At heart, the educated person is a sense-maker, that is, one who can wrest as much meaning as possible from her or his experiences.

It is amazing that Dewey can cover so many topics in such a small space. Reading "Creed" is like looking at a far-off star through a telescope. The telescope gives one a relatively clear view of the star, but shows little of the evening sky. In effect, "Creed" is a statement, written before the fact, of the conclusions of Dewey's argument. "Creed" tells what Dewey thinks but omits the "sky" that frames those conclusions.

In order to see that sky, in order to deal with Dewey's arguments for his educational conclusions, one should look at Dewey's magnum opus, *Democracy and Education*. Here, Dewey unpacks what he means by education and relates education to democracy. In a move typical of Dewey, he suggests that as much as we educate for democracy, we should democratize for education.

Finally, it is hard to overstate Dewey's influence in American schooling from the turn of the twentieth century through the 1930s. During that period, all sorts of progressive educational experiments and programs were espoused and tried. In New York, people set up schools where children were allowed to do as they pleased and to devise their own curricula. At the same time, progressive educators like George S. Counts were urging teachers to indoctrinate children with proper social ideals and values. Everybody, however, claimed John Dewey as a special influence. This led a somewhat exasperated Dewey to publish, in 1937, *Experience and Education*. There he tried to make explicit his own brand of progressivism and to correct the excesses of many of his followers.

In *Experience and Education*, Dewey reiterates his opposition to either/or thinking. Specifically, Dewey rejects the either/or (Platonic/Aristotelian) worldview that dominated the Western world for so long. From this rather traditional perspective, knowledge is either innate—inside the individual at birth awaiting the right mnemonic device to bring it to consciousness—or external to human beings, awaiting our discovery. In either case, an absolute is implied, resulting in the imposition of knowledge and values upon each new generation. Such a worldview may be appropriate for a monarchy or some other form of autocracy, but it is antithetical to education in a democracy.

Is rejection enough? Is the urge to destroy really—as Bakunin suggests—a creative urge? Dewey realizes that if the so-called new education is developed as a negative reaction to traditional beliefs, then its advocates have fallen into the trap of either/or thinking. All too often what occurred in Dewey's name and under the rubric of progressivism was nothing more than mere reaction to the authorities of the past, with little or no attempt to reconstruct that which had been torn down. While such deconstruction may be necessary, it is not sufficient. For Dewey, there must be a vision of a better way, a more appropriate way for improving the individual within the collective, the human being in society.

In writing *Experience and Education*, Dewey suggested that many so-called progressives built their "new education" as a negative reaction to that which they did not like or with which they did not agree. Rather than just rebelling against the traditional version of either/or thinking, Dewey based his "new education" on experience. In distinguishing good or educative experiences from bad or miseducative experiences, Dewey suggests that good experience is characterized by both interaction and continuity. An educative experience is one in which an active mind interacts with a wide-open world to solve genuine problems that are continuous with, yet different from, previous experiences. Recognizing that we are creatures of habit,

Dewey suggests that it is our unique ability to stop, reflect, and then act—that is, to respond intelligently to a problematic situation requiring more than a mere habitual reaction—that distinguishes humans from less intelligent animals. In *Experience and Education,* Dewey offers the reader a succinct yet clear explanation of what he means by experience and how the key elements of interaction and continuity complement one another in good or educative experiences.

A careful reading of *Experience and Education* offers insights into Dewey's view of democracy. As already noted, Dewey championed democracy throughout his long life, and democracy for Dewey was more than opposition to authoritarian rule. Dewey was no anarchist. The basis for authority in a democracy is experience. Dewey suggests that in a true democracy, "it is not the will or desire of any one person (a philosopher-king or scientist) which establishes order but the moving spirit of the whole group." Creating and sustaining such a "moving spirit" is in Dewey's mind what education and philosophy should be about.

The poet Allen Ginsberg urged readers to "be not too quick to understand" his friend, the novelist Jack Kerouac. A similar caution ought to be adopted with John Dewey. A superficial reading of Article I of "Creed" might suggest that Dewey is trying to "adjust" the student to society. An equally superficial reading of Article V might suggest that Dewey is trying to overthrow the existing society. Dewey, unless he contradicts himself cannot be doing both. The excerpts from *Democracy and Education* and *Experience and Education* are meant to be the first steps in helping the reader to discover what Dewey meant and to formulate for herself or himself what education is.

Notes

1. Robert B. Westbrook, *John Dewey and American Democracy* (Ithaca: Cornell University Press, 1991), p. 203.
2. Ibid., p. vi.
3. Ibid., p. 536.
4. This quotation as well as much of the information in this brief introduction were derived from John Novak's review (distributed by the John Dewey Society) of John Westbrook's *John Dewey and American Democracy.*

"My Pedagogic Creed" (1897)

Article I—*What Education Is*

I believe that

—all education proceeds by the participation of the individual in the social consciousness of the race. This process begins unconsciously almost at birth,

From *John Dewey: The Early Works 1895–1898, vol. 5,* Jo Ann Boydston (Ed.) (Carbondale, IL: Southern Illinois University Press, © 1972), pp. 84–95. Reprinted by permission of Southern Illinois University Press.

and is continually shaping the individual's powers, saturating his consciousness, forming his habits, training his ideas, and arousing his feelings and emotions. Through this unconscious education the individual gradually comes to share in the intellectual and moral resources which humanity has succeeded in getting together. He becomes an inheritor of the funded capital of civilization. The most formal and technical education in the world cannot safely depart from this general process. It can only organize it or differentiate it in some particular direction.

—the only true education comes through the stimulation of the child's powers by the demands of the social situations in which he finds himself. Through these demands he is stimulated to act as a member of a unity, to emerge from his original narrowness of action and feeling, and to conceive of himself from the standpoint of the welfare of the group to which he belongs. Through the responses which others make to his own activities he comes to know what these mean in social terms. The value which they have is reflected back into them. For instance, through the response which is made to the child's instinctive babblings the child comes to know what those babblings mean; they are transformed into articulate language, and thus the child is introduced into the consolidated wealth of ideas and emotions which are now summed up in language.

—this educational process has two sides—one psychological and one sociological—and that neither can be subordinated to the other, or neglected, without evil results following. Of these two sides, the psychological is the basis. The child's own instincts and powers furnish the material and give the starting-point for all education. Save as the efforts of the educator connect with some activity which the child is carrying on of his own initiative independent of the educator, education becomes reduced to a pressure from without. It may, indeed, give certain external results, but cannot truly be called educative. Without insight into the psychological structure and activities of the individual, the educative process will, therefore, be haphazard and arbitrary. If it chances to coincide with the child's activity it will get a leverage; if it does not, it will result in friction, or disintegration, or arrest of the child nature.

—knowledge of social conditions, of the present state of civilization, is necessary in order properly to interpret the child's powers. The child has his own instincts and tendencies, but we do not know what these mean until we can translate them into their social equivalents. We must be able to carry them back into a social past and see them as the inheritance of previous race activities. We must also be able to project them into the future to see what their outcome and end will be. In the illustration just used, it is the ability to see in the child's babblings the promise and potency of a future social intercourse and conversation which enables one to deal in the proper way with that instinct.

—the psychological and social sides are organically related, and that education cannot be regarded as a compromise between the two, or a superimposition of one upon the other. We are told that the psychological definition of education is barren and formal—that it gives us only the idea of a development of all the mental powers without giving us any idea of the use to which these powers are put. On the other hand, it is urged that the social definition of education, as getting adjusted to civilization, makes of it a forced and external process, and results in subordinating the freedom of the individual to a preconceived social and political status.

—each of these objections is true when urged against one side isolated from the other. In order to know what a power really is we must know what its end, use, or function is, and this we cannot know save as we conceive of the individual as active in social relationships. But, on the other hand, the only possible adjustment which we can give to the child under existing conditions is that which arises through putting him in complete possession of all his powers. With the advent of democracy and modern industrial conditions, it is impossible to foretell definitely just what civilization will be twenty years from now. Hence it is impossible to prepare the child for any precise set of conditions. To prepare him for the future life means to give him command of himself; it means so to train him that he will have the full and ready use of all his capacities; that his eye and ear and hand may be tools ready to command, that his judgment may be capable of grasping the conditions under which it has to work, and the executive forces be trained to act economically and efficiently. It is impossible to reach this sort of adjustment save as constant regard is had to the individual's own powers, tastes, and interests—that is, as education is continually converted into psychological terms.

In sum, I believe that the individual who is to be educated is a social individual, and that society is an organic union of individuals. If we eliminate the social factor from the child we are left only with an abstraction; if we eliminate the individual factor from society, we are left only with an inert and lifeless mass. Education, therefore, must begin with a psychological insight into the child's capacities, interests, and habits. It must be controlled at every point by reference to these same considerations. These powers, interests, and habits must be continually interpreted—we must know what they mean. They must be translated into terms of their social equivalents—into terms of what they are capable of in the way of social service.

Article II—*What The School Is*

I believe that

—the school is primarily a social institution. Education being a social process, the school is simply that form of community life in which all those agencies are concentrated that will be most effective in bringing the child to share in the inherited resources of the race, and to use his own powers for social ends.

—education, therefore, is a process of living and not a preparation for future living.

—the school must represent present life—life as real and vital to the child as that which he carries on in the home, in the neighborhood, or on the playground.

—that education which does not occur through forms of life, forms that are worth living for their own sake, is always a poor substitute for the genuine reality, and tends to cramp and to deaden.

—the school, as an institution, should simplify existing social life; should reduce it, as it were, to an embryonic form. Existing life is so complex that the child cannot be brought into contact with it without either confusion or distraction; he is either overwhelmed by the multiplicity of activities which are going on, so that he loses his own power of orderly reaction, or he is so stimulated by these various activities that his powers are prematurely called into play and he becomes either unduly specialized or else disintegrated.

—as such simplified social life, the school life should grow gradually out of the home life; that it should take up and continue the activities with which the child is already familiar in the home.

—it should exhibit these activities to the child, and reproduce them in such ways that the child will gradually learn the meaning of them, and be capable of playing his own part in relation to them.

—this is a psychological necessity, because it is the only way of securing continuity in the child's growth, the only way of giving a background of past experience to the new ideas given in school.

—it is also a social necessity because the home is the form of social life in which the child has been nurtured and in connection with which he has had his moral training. It is the business of the school to deepen and extend his sense of the values bound up in his home life.

—much of present education fails because it neglects this fundamental principle of the school as a form of community life. It conceives the school as a place where certain information is to be given, where certain lessons are to be learned, or where certain habits are to be formed. The value of these is conceived as lying largely in the remote future; the child must do these things for the sake of something else he is to do; they are mere preparations. As a result they do not become a part of the life experience of the child and so are not truly educative.

—the moral education centers upon this conception of the school as a mode of social life, that the best and deepest moral training is precisely that which one gets through having to enter into proper relations with others in a unity of work and thought. The present educational systems, so far as they destroy or neglect this unity, render it difficult or impossible to get any genuine, regular moral training.

—the child should be stimulated and controlled in his work through the life of the community.

—under existing conditions far too much of the stimulus and control proceeds from the teacher, because of neglect of the idea of the school as a form of social life.

—the teacher's place and work in the school is to be interpreted from this same basis. The teacher is not in the school to impose certain ideas or to form certain habits in the child, but is there as a member of the community to select the influences which shall affect the child and to assist him in properly responding to these influences.

—the discipline of the school should proceed from the life of the school as a whole and not directly from the teacher.

—the teacher's business is simply to determine, on the basis of larger experience and riper wisdom, how the discipline of life shall come to the child.

—all questions of the grading of the child and his promotion should be determined by reference to the same standard. Examinations are of use only so far as they test the child's fitness for social life and reveal the place in which he can be of the most service and where he can receive the most help.

Article III—*The Subject-Matter of Education*

I believe that

—the social life of the child is the basis of concentration, or correlation, in all his training or growth. The social life gives the unconscious unity and the background of all his efforts and of all his attainments.

—the subject-matter of the school curriculum should mark a gradual differentiation out of the primitive unconscious unity of social life.

—we violate the child's nature and render difficult the best ethical results by introducing the child too abruptly to a number of special studies, of reading, writing, geography, etc., out of relation to this social life.

—the true center of correlation on the school subjects is not science, nor literature, nor history, nor geography, but the child's own social activities.

—education cannot be unified in the study of science, or so-called nature study, because apart from human activity, nature itself is not a unity; nature in itself is a number of diverse objects in space and time, and to attempt to make it the center of work by itself is to introduce a principle of radiation rather than one of concentration.

—literature is the reflex expression and interpretation of social experience; that hence it must follow upon and not precede such experience. It, therefore, cannot be made the basis, although it may be made the summary of unification.

—once more that history is of educative value in so far as it presents phases of social life and growth. It must be controlled by reference to social life. When taken simply as history it is thrown into the distant past and becomes dead and inert. Taken as the record of man's social life and progress it becomes full of meaning. I believe, however, that it cannot be so taken excepting as the child is also introduced directly into social life.

—the primary basis of education is in the child's powers at work along the same general constructive lines as those which have brought civilization into being.

—the only way to make the child conscious of his social heritage is to enable him to perform those fundamental types of activity which make civilization what it is.

—in the so-called expressive or constructive activities as the center of correlation.

—this gives the standard for the place of cooking, sewing, manual training, etc., in the school.

—they are not special studies which are to be introduced over and above a lot of others in the way of relaxation or relief, or as additional accomplishments. I believe rather that they represent, as types, fundamental forms of social activity; and that it is possible and desirable that the child's introduction into the more formal subjects of the curriculum be through the medium of these activities.

—the study of science is educational in so far as it brings out the materials and processes which make social life what it is.

—one of the greatest difficulties in the present teaching of science is that the material is presented in purely objective form, or is treated as a new peculiar kind of experience which the child can add to that which he has already had. In reality, science is of value because it gives the ability to interpret and control the experience already had. It should be introduced, not as so much new subject-matter, but as showing the factors already involved in previous experience and as furnishing tools by which that experience can be more easily and effectively regulated.

—at present we lose much of the value of literature and language studies because of our elimination of the social element. Language is almost always treated in the books of pedagogy simply as the expression of thought. It is true that language is a logical instrument, but it is fundamentally and primarily a social instrument. Language is the device for communication; it is the tool through which one individual comes to share the ideas and feelings of others. When treated simply as a way of getting individual information, or as a means of showing off what one has learned, it loses its social motive and end.

—there is, therefore, no succession of studies in the ideal school curriculum. If education is life, all life has, from the outset, a scientific aspect, an aspect of art and culture, and an aspect of communication. It cannot, therefore, be true that the proper studies for one grade are mere reading and writing, and that at a later grade, reading, or literature, or science, may be introduced. The progress is not in the succession of studies, but in the development of new attitudes towards, and new interests in, experience.

—education must be conceived as a continuing reconstruction of experience; that the process and the goal of education are one and the same thing.

—to set up any end outside of education, as furnishing its goal and standard, is to deprive the educational process of much of its meaning, and tends to make us rely upon false and external stimuli in dealing with the child.

Article IV—*The Nature of Method*

I believe that

—the question of method is ultimately reducible to the question of the order of development of the child's powers and interests. The law for presenting and treating material is the law implicit within the child's own nature. Because this is so I believe the following statements are of supreme importance as determining the spirit in which education is carried on:

—the active side precedes the passive in the development of the child-nature; that expression comes before conscious impression; that the muscular development precedes the sensory; that movements come before conscious sensations; I believe that consciousness is essentially motor or impulsive; that conscious states tend to project themselves in action.

—the neglect of this principle is the cause of a large part of the waste of time and strength in school work. The child is thrown into a passive, receptive, or absorbing attitude. The conditions are such that he is not permitted to follow the law of his nature; the result is friction and waste.

—ideas (intellectual and rational processes) also result from action and devolve for the sake of the better control of action. What we term reason is primarily the law of orderly or effective action. To attempt to develop the reasoning powers, the powers of judgment, without reference to the selection and arrangement of means in action, is the fundamental fallacy in our present methods of dealing with this matter. As a result we present the child with arbitrary symbols. Symbols are a necessity in mental development, but they have their place as tools for economizing effort; presented by themselves they are a mass of meaningless and arbitrary ideas imposed from without.

—the image is the great instrument of instruction. What a child gets out of any subject presented to him is simply the images which he himself forms with regard to it.

—if nine-tenths of the energy at present directed towards making the child learn certain things were spent in seeing to it that the child was forming proper images, the work of instruction would be indefinitely facilitated.

—much of the time and attention now given to the preparation and presentation of lessons might be more wisely and profitably expended in training the child's power of imagery and in seeing to it that he was continually forming definite, vivid, and growing images of the various subjects with which he comes in contact in his experience.

—interests are the signs and symptoms of growing power. I believe that they represent dawning capacities. Accordingly the constant and careful observation of interests is of the utmost importance for the educator.

—these interests are to be observed as showing the state of development which the child has reached.

—they prophesy the stage upon which he is about to enter.

—only through the continual and sympathetic observation of childhood's interests can the adult enter into the child's life and see what it is ready for, and upon what material it could work most readily and fruitfully.

—these interests are neither to be humored nor repressed. To repress interest is to substitute the adult for the child, and so to weaken intellectual curiosity and alertness, to suppress initiative, and to deaden interest. To humor the interests is to substitute the transient for the permanent. The interest is always the sign of some power below; the important thing is to discover this power. To humor the interest is to fail to penetrate below the surface, and its sure result is to substitute caprice and whim for genuine interest.

—the emotions are the reflex of actions.

—to endeavor to stimulate or arouse the emotions apart from their corresponding activities is to introduce an unhealthy and morbid state of mind.

—if we can only secure right habits of action and thought, with reference to the good, the true, and the beautiful, the emotions will for the most part take care of themselves.

—next to deadness and dullness, formalism and routine, our education is threatened with no greater evil than sentimentalism.

—this sentimentalism is the necessary result of the attempt to divorce feeling from action.

Article V—*The School and Social Progress*

I believe that

—education is the fundamental method of social progress and reform.

—all reforms which rest simply upon the enactment of law, or the threatening of certain penalties, or upon changes in mechanical or outward arrangements, are transitory and futile.

—education is a regulation of the process of coming to share in the social consciousness; and that the adjustment of individual activity on the basis of this social consciousness is the only sure method of social reconstruction.

—this conception has due regard for both the individualistic and socialistic ideals. It is duly individual because it recognizes the formation of a certain character as the only genuine basis of right living. It is socialistic because it recognizes that this right character is not to be formed by merely individual precept, example, or exhortation, but rather by the influence of a certain form of institutional or community life upon the individual, and that the social organism through the school, as its organ, may determine ethical results.

—in the ideal school we have the reconciliation of the individualistic and the institutional ideals.

—the community's duty to education is, therefore, its paramount moral duty. By law and punishment, by social agitation and discussion, society can regulate and form itself in a more or less haphazard and chance way. But through education society can formulate its own purposes, can organize its own means and resources, and thus shape itself with definiteness and economy in the direction in which it wishes to move.

—when society once recognizes the possibilities in this direction, and the obligations which these possibilities impose, it is impossible to conceive of the resources of time, attention, and money which will be put at the disposal of the educator.

—it is the business of every one interested in education to insist upon the school as the primary and most effective interest of social progress and reform in order that society may be awakened to realize what the school stands for, and aroused to the necessity of endowing the educator with sufficient equipment properly to perform his task.

—education thus conceived marks the most perfect and intimate union of science and art conceivable in human experience.

—the art of thus giving shape to human powers and adapting them to social service is the supreme art; one calling into its service the best of artists; that no insight, sympathy, tact, executive power, is too great for such service.

—with the growth of psychological service, giving added insight into individual structure and laws of growth; and with growth of social science, adding to our knowledge of the right organization of individuals, all scientific resources can be utilized for the purposes of education.

—when science and art thus join hands the most commanding motive for human action will be reached, the most genuine springs of human conduct aroused, and the best service that human nature is capable of guaranteed.

—the teacher is engaged, not simply in the training of individuals, but in the formation of the proper social life.

—every teacher should realize the dignity of his calling; that he is a social servant set apart for the maintenance of proper social order and the securing of the right social growth.

—in this way the teacher always is the prophet of the true God and the usherer in of the true kingdom of God.

From *Democracy and Education* (1916)

For the most part, save incidentally, we have hitherto been concerned with education as it may exist in any social group. We have now to make explicit the differences in the spirit, material, and method of education as it operates in different types of community life. To say that education is a social function, securing direction and development in the immature through their participation in the life of the group to which they belong, is to say in effect that education will vary with the quality of life which prevails in a group. Particularly is it true that a society which not only changes but which has the ideal of such

From *Democracy and Education* by John Dewey (NY: Macmillan Publishing, 1916).

change as will improve it, will have different standards and methods of education from one which aims simply at the perpetuation of its own customs. To make the general ideas set forth applicable to our own educational practice, it is, therefore, necessary to come to closer quarters with the nature of present social life.

1. The Implications of Human Association. Society is one word, but many things. Men associate together in all kinds of ways and for all kinds of purposes. One man is concerned in a multitude of diverse groups, in which his associates may be quite different. It often seems as if they had nothing in common except that they are modes of associated life. Within every larger social organization there are numerous minor groups: not only political subdivisions, but industrial, scientific, religious associations. There are political parties with differing aims, social sets, cliques, gangs, corporations, partnerships, groups bound closely together by ties of blood, and so on in endless variety. In many modern states and in some ancient, there is great diversity of populations, of varying languages, religions, moral codes, and traditions. From this standpoint, many a minor political unit, one of our large cities, for example, is a congeries of loosely associated societies, rather than an inclusive and permeating community of action and thought.

The terms of society, community, are thus ambiguous. They have both a eulogistic or normative sense, and a descriptive sense; a meaning *de jure* and a meaning *de facto*. In social philosophy, the former connotation is almost always uppermost. Society is conceived as one by its very nature. The qualities which accompany this unity, praiseworthy community of purpose and welfare, loyalty to public ends, mutuality of sympathy, are emphasized. But when we look at the facts which the term *denotes* instead of confining our attention to its intrinsic *connotation,* we find not unity, but a plurality of societies, good and bad. Men banded together in a criminal conspiracy, business aggregations that prey upon the public while serving it, political machines held together by the interest of plunder, are included. If it is said that such organizations are not societies because they do not meet the ideal requirements of the notion of society, the answer, in part, is that the conception of society is then made so "ideal" as to be of no use, having no reference to facts; and in part, that each of these organizations, no matter how opposed to the interests of other groups, has some thing of the praiseworthy qualities of "Society" which hold it together. There is honor among thieves, and a band of robbers has a common interest as respects its members. Gangs are marked by fraternal feeling, and narrow cliques by intense loyalty to their own codes. Family life may be marked by exclusiveness, suspicion, and jealousy as to those without, and yet be a model of amity and mutual aid within. Any education given by a group tends to socialize its members, but the quality and value of the socialization depends upon the habits and aims of the group.

Hence, once more, the need of a measure for the worth of any given mode of social life. In seeking this measure, we have to avoid two extremes. We can not set up, out of our heads, something we regard as an ideal society. We must base our conception upon societies which actually exist, in order to have any assurance that our ideal is a practicable one. But, as we have just seen, the ideal cannot simply repeat the traits which are actually found. The problem is to extract the desirable traits of forms of community life which actually exist, and employ them to criticize undesirable features and suggest improvement. Now in any social group whatever, even in a gang of thieves, we find some interest held in common, and we find a certain amount of interaction and coöperative intercourse with other groups. From these two traits we derive our standard. How numerous and varied are the interests which are consciously shared? How full and free is the interplay with other forms of association? If we apply these considerations to, say, a criminal band, we find that the ties which consciously hold the members together are few in number, reducible almost to a common interest in plunder; and that they are of such a nature as to isolate the group from other groups with respect to give and take of the values of life. Hence, the education such a society gives is partial and distorted. If we take, on the other hand, the kind of family life which illustrates the standard, we find that there are material, intellectual, aesthetic interests in which all participate and that the progress of one member has worth for the experience of other members—it is readily communicable—and that the family is not an isolated whole, but enters intimately into relationships with business groups, with schools, with all the agencies of culture, as well as with other similar groups, and that it plays a due part in the political organization and in return receives support from it. In short, there are many interests consciously communicated and shared; and there are varied and free points of contact with other modes of association.

I. Let us apply the first element in this criterion to a despotically governed state. It is not true there is no common interest in such an organization between governed and governors. The authorities in command must make some appeal to the native activities of the subjects, must call some of their powers into play. Talleyrand said that a government could do everything with bayonets except sit on them. This cynical declaration is at least a recognition that the bond of union is not merely one of coercive force. It may be said, however, that the activities appealed to are themselves unworthy and degrading—that such a government calls into functioning activity simply capacity for fear. In a way, this statement is true. But it overlooks the fact that fear need not be an undesirable factor in experience. Caution, circumspection, prudence, desire to foresee future events so as to avert what is harmful, these desirable traits are as much a product of calling the impulse of fear into play as is cowardice and abject submission. The real difficulty is that the appeal to fear is *isolated*. In evoking dread and hope of specific tangible reward—say comfort and ease—many other capacities are left untouched. Or rather, they are affected, but in such a way as to pervert them. Instead of operating on their own account they are reduced to mere servants of attaining pleasure and avoiding pain.

This is equivalent to saying that there is no extensive number of common interests; there is no free play back and forth among the members of the social group. Stimulation and response are exceedingly one-sided. In order to have a larger number of values in common, all the members of the group must have an equable opportunity to receive and to take from others. There must be a large variety of shared undertakings and experiences. Otherwise, the influences which educate some into masters, educate others into slaves. And the experience of each party loses in meaning, when the free interchange of varying modes of life-experience is arrested. A separation into a privileged and a subject-class prevents social endosmosis. The evils thereby affecting the superior class are less material and less perceptible, but equally real. Their culture tends to be sterile, to be turned back to feed on itself; their art becomes a showy display and artificial; their wealth luxurious; their knowledge overspecialized; their manners fastidious rather than humane.

Lack of the free and equitable intercourse which springs from a variety of shared interests makes intellectual stimulation unbalanced. Diversity of stimulation means novelty, and novelty means challenge to thought. The more activity is restricted to a few definite lines—as it is when there are rigid class lines preventing adequate interplay of experiences—the more action tends to become routine on the part of the class at a disadvantage, and capricious, aimless, and explosive on the part of the class having the materially fortunate position. Plato defined a slave as one who accepts from another the purposes which control his conduct. This condition obtains even where there is no slavery in the legal sense. It is found wherever men are engaged in activity which is socially serviceable, but whose service they do not understand and have no personal interest in. Much is said about scientific management of work. It is a narrow view which restricts the science which secures efficiency of operation to movements of the muscles. The chief opportunity for science is the discovery of the relations of a man to his work—including his relations to others who take part—which will enlist his intelligent interest in what he is doing. Efficiency in production often demands division of labor. But it is reduced to a mechanical routine unless workers see the technical, intellectual, and social relationships involved in what they do, and engage in their work because of the motivation furnished by such perceptions. The tendency to reduce such things as efficiency of activity and scientific management to purely technical externals is evidence of the one-sided stimulation of thought given to those in control of industry—those who supply its aims. Because of their lack of all-round and well-balanced social interest, there is not sufficient stimulus for attention to the human factors and relationships in industry. Intelligence is narrowed to the factors concerned with technical production and marketing of goods. No doubt, a very acute and intense intelligence in these narrow lines can be developed, but the failure to take into account the significant social factors means none the less an absence of mind, and a corresponding distortion of emotional life.

II. This illustration (whose point is to be extended to all associations lacking reciprocity of interest) brings us to our second point. The isolation and exclusiveness of a gang or clique brings its antisocial spirit into relief. But this same spirit is found wherever one group has interests "of its own" which shut it out from full interaction with other groups, so that its prevailing purpose is the protection of what it has got, instead of reorganization and progress through wider relationships. It marks nations in their isolation from one another; families which seclude their domestic concerns as if they had no connection with a larger life; schools when separated from the interest of home and community; the divisions of rich and poor; learned and unlearned. The essential point is that isolation makes for rigidity and formal institutionalizing of life, for static and selfish ideals within the group. That savage tribes regard aliens and enemies as synonymous is not accidental. It springs from the fact that they have identified their experience with rigid adherence to their past customs. On such a basis it is wholly logical to fear intercourse with others, for such contact might dissolve custom. It would certainly occasion reconstruction. It is a commonplace that an alert and expanding mental life depends upon an enlarging range of contact with the physical environment. But the principle applies even more significantly to the field where we are apt to ignore it—the sphere of social contacts.

Every expansive era in the history of mankind has coincided with the operation of factors which have tended to eliminate distance between peoples and classes previously hemmed off from one another. Even the alleged benefits of war, so far as more than alleged, spring from the fact that conflict of peoples at least enforces intercourse between them and thus accidentally enables them to learn from one another, and thereby to expand their horizons. Travel, economic and commercial tendencies, have at present gone far to break down external barriers; to bring peoples and classes into closer and more perceptible connection with one another. It remains for the most part to secure the intellectual and emotional significance of this physical annihilation of space.

2. The Democratic Ideal. The two elements in our criterion both point to democracy. The first signifies not only more numerous and more varied points of shared common interest, but greater reliance upon the recognition of mutual interests as a factor in social control. The second means not only freer interaction between social groups (once isolated so far as intention could keep up a separation) but change in social habit—its continuous readjustment through meeting the new situations produced by varied intercourse. And these two traits are precisely what characterize the democratically constituted society.

Upon the educational side, we note first that the realization of a form of social life in which interests are mutually interpenetrating, and where progress, or readjustment, is an important consideration, makes a democratic community more interested than other communities have cause to be in deliberate and systematic education. The devotion of democracy to education is a familiar fact. The superficial explanation is that a government resting upon popular suffrage cannot be successful unless those who elect and who obey their governors are educated. Since a democratic society repudiates the principle of external authority, it must find a substitute in voluntary disposition and interest; these can be created only by education. But there is a deeper explanation. A democracy is more than a form of government; it is primarily a mode of associated living, of conjoint communicated experience. The extension in space of the number of individuals who participate in an interest so that each has to refer his own action to that of others, and to consider the action of others to give point and direction to his own, is equivalent to the breaking down of those barriers of class, race, and national territory which kept men from perceiving the full import of their activity. These more numerous and more varied points of contact denote a greater diversity of stimuli to which an individual has to respond; they consequently put a premium on variation in his action. They secure a liberation of powers which remain suppressed as long as the incitations to action are partial, as they must be in a group which in its exclusiveness shuts out many interests.

The widening of the area of shared concerns, and the liberation of a greater diversity of personal capacities which characterize a democracy, are not of course the product of deliberation and conscious effort. On the contrary, they were caused by the development of modes of manufacture and commerce, travel, migration, and intercommunication which flowed from the command of science over natural energy. But after greater individualization on one hand and a broader community of interest on the other have come into existence it is a matter of deliberate effort to sustain and extend them. Obviously a society to which stratification into separate classes would be fatal, must see to it that intellectual opportunities are accessible to all on equable anal easy terms. A society marked off into classes need be specially attentive only to the education of its ruling elements. A society which is mobile, which is full of channels for the distribution of a change occurring anywhere, must see to it that its members are educated to personal initiative and adaptability. Otherwise they will be overwhelmed by the changes in which they are caught and whose significance or connections they do not perceive. The result will be a confusion in which a few will appropriate to themselves the results of the blind and externally directed activities of others.

From *Experience and Education* (1938)

If there is any truth in what has been said about the need of forming a theory of experience in order that education may be intelligently conducted upon the basis of experience, it is clear that the next thing in order in this discussion is to present the principles that are most significant in framing this theory. I shall not, therefore, apologize for engaging in a certain amount of philosophical analysis, which otherwise might be out of place. I may, however, reassure you to some degree by saying that this analysis is not an end in itself but is engaged in for the sake of obtaining criteria to be applied later in discussion of a number of concrete and, to most persons, more interesting issues.

I have already mentioned what I called the category of continuity, or the experiential continuum. This principle is involved, as I pointed out, in every attempt to discriminate between experiences that are worth while educationally and those that are not. It may seem superfluous to argue that this discrimination is necessary not only in criticizing the traditional type of education but

From *Experience and Education* by John Dewey (IN: Kappa Delta Pi, © 1938), pp. 33–50. Reprinted by permission of Kappa Delta Pi, an International Honor Society in Education.

also in initiating and conducting a different type. Nevertheless, it is advisable to pursue for a little while the idea that it is necessary. One may safely assume, I suppose, that one thing which has recommended the progressive movement is that it seems more in accord with the democratic ideal to which our people is committed than do the procedures of the traditional school, since the latter have so much of the autocratic about them. Another thing which has contributed to its favorable reception is that its methods are humane in comparison with the harshness so often attending the policies of the traditional school.

The question I would raise concerns why we prefer democratic and humane arrangements to those which are autocratic and harsh. And by "why," I mean the *reason* for preferring them, not just the *causes* which lead us to the preference. One *cause* may be that we have been taught not only in the schools but by the press, the pulpit, the platform, and our laws and law-making bodies that democracy is the best of all social institutions. We may have so assimilated this idea from our surroundings that it has become an habitual part of our mental and moral make-up. But similar causes have led other persons in different surroundings to widely varying conclusions—to prefer fascism, for example. The cause for our preference is not the same thing as the reason why we *should* prefer it.

It is not my purpose here to go in detail into the reason. But I would ask a single question: Can we find any reason that does not ultimately come down to the belief that democratic social arrangements promote a better quality of human experience, one which is more widely accessible and enjoyed, than do non-democratic and anti-democratic forms of social life? Does not the principle of regard for individual freedom and for decency and kindliness of human relations come back in the end to the conviction that these things are tributary to a higher quality of experience on the part of a greater number than are methods of repression and coercion or force? Is it not the reason for our preference that we believe that mutual consultation and convictions reached through persuasion make possible a better quality of experience than can otherwise be provided on any wide scale?

If the answer to these questions is in the affirmative (and personally I do not see how we can justify our preference for democracy and humanity on any other ground), the ultimate reason for hospitality to progressive education, because of its reliance upon and use of humane methods and its kinship to democracy, goes back to the fact that discrimination is made between the inherent values of different experiences. So I come back to the principle of continuity of experience as a criterion of discrimination.

At bottom, this principle rests upon the fact of habit, when *habit* is interpreted biologically. The basic characteristic of habit is that every experience enacted and undergone modifies the one who acts and undergoes, while this modification affects, whether we wish it or not, the quality of subsequent experiences. For it is a somewhat different person who enters into them. The principle of habit so understood obviously goes deeper than the ordinary conception of *a* habit as a more or less fixed way of doing things, although it includes the latter as one of its special cases. It covers the formation of attitudes, attitudes that are emotional and intellectual; it covers our basic sensitivities and ways of meeting and responding to all the conditions which we meet in living. From this point of view, the principle of continuity of experience means that every experience both takes up something from those which have gone before and modifies in some way the quality of those which come after. As the poet states it,

> . . . all experience is an arch wherethro'
> Gleams that untraveled world, whose margin fades
> For ever and for ever when I move.

So far, however, we have no ground for discrimination among experiences. For the principle is of universal application. There is *some* kind of continuity in every case. It is when we note the different forms in which continuity of experience operates that we get the basis of discriminating among experiences. I may illustrate what is meant by an objection which has been brought against an idea which I once put forth—namely, that the educative process can be identified with growth when that is understood in terms of the active participle, *growing*.

Growth, or growing as developing, not only physically but intellectually and morally, is one exemplification of the principle of continuity. The objection made is that growth might take many different directions: a man, for example, who starts out on a career of burglary may grow in that direction, and by practice may grow into a highly expert burglar. Hence it is argued that "growth" is not enough; we must also specify the direction in which growth takes place, the end towards which it tends. Before, however, we decide that the objection is conclusive we must analyze the case a little further.

That a man may grow in efficiency as a burglar, as a gangster, or as a corrupt politician, cannot be doubted. But from the standpoint of growth as education and education as growth the question is whether growth in this direction promotes or retards growth in general. Does this form of growth create conditions for further growth, or does it set up conditions that shut off the person who has grown in this particular direction from the occasions, stimuli, and opportunities for continuing growth in new directions? What is the effect of growth in a special direction upon the attitudes and habits which alone open up avenues for development in other lines? I shall leave you to answer these questions, saying simply that when and *only* when development in a particular line conduces to continuing growth does it answer to the criterion of education as growing. For the conception is one that must find universal and not specialized limited application.

I return now to the question of continuity as a criterion by which to discriminate between experiences which are educative and those which are miseducative. As we have seen, there is some kind of continuity in any case since every experience affects for better or worse the attitudes which help decide the quality of further experiences, by setting up certain preference and aversion, and making it easier or harder to act for this or that end. Moreover, every experience influences in some degree the objective conditions under which further experiences are had. For example, a child who learns to speak has a new facility and new desire. But he has also widened the external conditions of subsequent learning. When he learns to read, he similarly opens up a new environment. If a person decides to become a teacher, lawyer, physician, or stockbroker, when he executes his intention he thereby necessarily determines to some extent the environment in which he will act in the future. He has rendered himself more sensitive and responsive to certain conditions, and relatively immune to those things about him that would have been stimuli if he had made another choice.

But, while the principle of continuity applies in some way in every case, the quality of the present experience influences the *way* in which the principle applies. We speak of spoiling a child and of the spoilt child. The effect of overindulging a child is a continuing one. It sets up an attitude which operates as an automatic demand that persons and objects cater to his desires and caprices in the future. It makes him seek the kind of situation that will enable him to do what he feels like doing at the time. It renders him averse to and comparatively incompetent in situations which require effort and perseverance in overcoming obstacles. There is no paradox in the fact that the principle of the continuity of experience may operate so as to leave a person arrested on a low plane of development, in a way which limits later capacity for growth.

On the other hand, if an experience arouses curiosity, strengthens initiative, and sets up desires and purposes that are sufficiently intense to carry a person over dead places in the future, continuity works in a very different way. Every experience is a moving force. Its value can be judged only on the ground of what it moves toward and into. The greater maturity of experience which should belong to the adult as educator puts him in a position to evaluate each experience of the young in a way in which the one having the less mature experience cannot do. It is then the business of the educator to see in what direction an experience is heading. There is no point in his being more mature if, instead of using his greater insight to help organize the conditions of the experience of the immature, he throws away his insight. Failure to take the moving force of an experience into account so as to judge and direct it on the ground of what it is moving into means disloyalty to the principle of experience itself. The disloyalty operates in two directions. The educator is false to the understanding that he should have obtained from his own past experience. He is also unfaithful to the fact that all human experience is ultimately social: that it involves contact and communication. The mature person, to put it in moral terms, has no right to withhold from the young on given occasions whatever capacity for sympathetic understanding his own experience has given him.

No sooner, however, are such things said than there is a tendency to react to the other extreme and take what has been said as a plea for some sort of disguised imposition from outside. It is worth while, accordingly, to say something about the way in which the adult can exercise the wisdom his own wider experience gives him without imposing a merely external control. On one side, it is his business to be on the alert to see what attitudes and habitual tendencies are being created. In this direction he must, if he is an educator, be able to judge what attitudes are actually conducive to continued growth and what are detrimental. He must, in addition, have that sympathetic understanding of individuals as individuals which gives him an idea of what is actually going on in the minds of those who are learning. It is, among other things, the need for these abilities on the part of the parent and teacher which makes a system of education based upon living experience a more difficult affair to conduct successfully than it is to follow the patterns of traditional education.

But there is another aspect of the matter. Experience does not go on simply inside a person. It does go on there, for it influences the formation of attitudes of desire and purpose. But this is not the whole of the story. Every genuine experience has an active side which changes in some degree the objective conditions under which experiences are had. The difference between civilization and savagery, to take an example on a large scale, is found in the degree in which previous experiences have changed the objective conditions under which subsequent experiences take place. The existence of roads, of means of rapid movement and transportation, tools, implements, furniture, electric light and power, are illustrations. Destroy the external conditions of present civilized experience, and for a time our experience would relapse into that of barbaric peoples.

In a word, we live from birth to death in a world of persons and things which in large measure is what it is because of what has been done and transmitted from previous human activities. When this fact is ignored, experience is treated as if it were something which goes on exclusively inside an individual's body and mind. It ought not to be necessary to say that experience does not occur in a vacuum. There are sources outside an individual which give rise to experience. It is constantly fed from these springs. No one would question that a child in a slum tenement has a different experience from that of a child in a cultured home; that the country lad has a different kind of experience from the city boy, or a boy on the seashore one different from the lad who is brought up on inland prairies. Ordinarily we take such facts for granted as too commonplace to record. But when their educational import is recognized, they indicate the second way in which the educator can direct the experience of the young without engaging in imposition. A primary responsibility of educators is that they not only be aware of the general principle of the shaping of actual experience by environing conditions, but that they also recognize in the concrete what surroundings are conducive to having experiences that lead to growth. Above all, they should know how to utilize the surroundings, physical and social, that exist so as to extract from them all that they have to contribute to building up experiences that are worth while.

Traditional education did not have to face this problem; it could systematically dodge this responsibility. The school environment of desks, blackboards, a small school yard, was supposed to suffice. There was no demand that the teacher should become intimately acquainted with the conditions of the local community, physical, historical, economic, occupational, etc., in order to utilize them as educational resources. A system of education based upon the necessary connection of education with experience must, on the contrary, if faithful to its principle, take these things constantly into account. This tax upon the educator is another reason why progressive education is more difficult to carry on than was ever the traditional system.

It is possible to frame schemes of education that pretty systematically subordinate objective conditions to those which reside in the individuals being educated. This happens whenever the place and function of the teacher, of books, of apparatus and equipment, of everything which represents the products of the more mature experience of elders, is systematically subordinated to the immediate inclinations and feelings of the young. Every theory which assumes that importance can be attached to these objective factors only at the expense of imposing external control and of limiting the freedom of individuals rests finally upon the notion that experience is truly experience only when objective conditions are subordinated to what goes on within the individuals having the experience.

I do not mean that it is supposed that objective conditions can be shut out. It is recognized that they must enter in: so much concession is made to the inescapable fact that we live in a world of things and persons. But I think that observation of what goes on in some families and some schools would disclose that some parents and some teachers are acting upon the idea of *subordinating* objective conditions to internal ones. In that case, it is assumed not only that the latter are primary, which in one sense they are, but that just as they temporarily exist they fix the whole educational process.

Let me illustrate from the case of an infant. The needs of a baby for food, rest, and activity are certainly primary and decisive in one respect. Nourishment must be provided; provision must be made for comfortable sleep, and so on. But these facts do not mean that a parent shall feed the baby at any time when the baby is cross or irritable, that there shall not be a program of regular hours of feeding and sleeping, etc. The wise mother takes account of the needs of the infant but not in a way which dispenses with her own responsibility for regulating the objective conditions under which the needs are satisfied. And if she is a wise mother in this respect, she draws upon past experiences of experts as well as her own for the light that these shed upon what experiences are in general most conducive to the normal development of infants. Instead of these conditions being subordinated to the immediate internal condition of the baby, they are definitely ordered so that a particular kind of *interaction* with these immediate internal states may be brought about.

The word "interaction," which has just been used, expresses the second chief principle for interpreting an experience in its educational function and force. It assigns equal rights to both factors in experience—objective and internal conditions. Any normal experience is an interplay of these two sets of conditions. Taken together, or in their interaction, they form what we call a *situation*. The trouble with traditional education was not that it emphasized the external conditions that enter into the control of the experiences but that it paid so little attention to the internal factors which also decide what kind of experience is had. It violated the principle of interaction from one side. But this violation is no reason why the new education should violate the principle from the other side—except upon the basis of the extreme *Either-Or* educational philosophy which has been mentioned.

The illustration drawn from the need for regulation of the objective conditions of a baby's development indicates, first, that the parent has responsibility for arranging the conditions under which an infant's experience of food, sleep, etc., occurs, and, secondly, that the responsibility is fulfilled by utilizing the funded experience of the past, as this is represented, say, by the advice of competent physicians and others who have made a special study of normal physical growth. Does it limit the freedom of the mother when she uses the body of knowledge thus provided to regulate the objective conditions of nourishment and sleep? Or does the enlargement of her intelligence in fulfilling her parental function widen her freedom? Doubtless if a fetish were made of the advice and directions so that they came to be inflexible dictates to be followed under every possible condition, then restriction of freedom of both parent and child would occur. But this restriction would also be a limitation of the intelligence that is exercised in personal judgment.

In what respect does regulation of objective conditions limit the freedom of the baby? Some limitation is certainly placed upon its immediate movements and inclinations when it is put in its crib, at a time when it wants to continue playing, or does not get food at the moment it would like it, or when it isn't picked up and dandled when it cries for attention. Restriction also occurs when mother or nurse snatches a child away from an open fire into which it is about to fall. I shall have more to say later about freedom. Here it is enough to ask whether freedom is to be thought of and adjudged on the basis of relatively momentary incidents or whether its meaning is found in the continuity of developing experience.

The statement that individuals live in a world means, in the concrete, that they live in a series of situations. And when it is said that they live *in* these situations, the meaning of the word "in" is different from its meaning when it is said that pennies are "in" a pocket or paint is "in" a can. It means, once more, that interaction is going on between an individual and objects and other persons. The conceptions of *situation* and of *interaction* are inseparable from each other. An experience is always what it is because of a transaction taking place between an individual and what, at the time, constitutes his environment, whether the latter consists of persons with whom he is talking about some topic or event, the subject talked about being also a part of the situation; or the toys with which he is playing; the book he is reading (in which his environing conditions at the time may be England or ancient Greece or an imaginary region); or the materials of an experiment he is performing. The environment, in other words, is whatever conditions interact with personal needs, desires, purposes, and capacities to create the experience which is had. Even when a person builds a castle in the air he is interacting with the objects which he constructs in fancy.

The two principles of continuity and interaction are not separate from each other. They intercept and unite. They are, so to speak, the longitudinal and lateral aspects of experience. Different situations succeed one another. But because of the principle of continuity something is carried over from the earlier to the later ones. As an individual passes from one situation to another, his world, his environment, expands or contracts. He does not find himself living in another world but in a different part or aspect of one and the same world. What he has learned in the way of knowledge and skill in one situation becomes an instrument of understanding and dealing effectively with the situations which follow. The process goes on as long as life and learning continue. Otherwise the course of experience is disorderly, since the individual factor that enters into making an experience is split. A divided world, a world whose parts and aspects do not hang together, is at once a sign and a cause of a divided personality. When the splitting-up reaches a certain point we call the person insane. A fully integrated personality, on the other hand, exists only when successive experiences are integrated with one another. It can be built up only as a world of related objects is constructed.

Continuity and interaction in their active union with each other provide the measure of the educative significance and value of an experience. The immediate and direct concern of an educator is then with the situations in which interaction takes place. The individual, who enters as a factor into it, is what he is at a given time. It is the other factor, that of objective conditions, which lies to some extent within the possibility of regulation by the educator. As has already been noted, the phrase "objective conditions" covers a wide range. It includes what is done by the educator and the way in which it is done, not only words spoken but the tone of voice in which they are spoken. It includes equipment, books, apparatus, toys, games played. It includes the materials with which an individual interacts, and, most important of all, the total *social* set-up of the situations in which a person is engaged.

When it is said that the objective conditions are those which are within the power of the educator to regulate, it is meant, of course, that his ability to influence directly the experience of others and thereby the education they obtain places upon him the duty of determining that environment which will interact with the existing capacities and needs of those taught to create a worth-while experience. The trouble with traditional education was not that educators took upon themselves the responsibility for providing an environment. The trouble was that they did not consider the other factor in creating an experience; namely, the powers and purposes of those taught. It was assumed that a certain set of conditions was intrinsically desirable, apart from its ability to evoke a certain quality of response in individuals. This lack of mutual adaptation made the process of teaching and learning accidental. Those to whom the provided conditions were suitable managed to learn. Others got on as best they could. Responsibility for selecting objective conditions carries with it, then, the responsibility for understanding the needs and capacities of the individuals who are learning at a given time. It is not enough that certain materials and methods have proved effective with other individuals at other times. There must be a reason for thinking that they will function in generating an experience that has educative quality with particular individuals at a particular time.

It is no reflection upon the nutritive quality of beefsteak that it is not fed to infants. It is not an invidious reflection upon trigonometry that we do not teach it in the first or fifth grade of school. It is not the subject *per se* that is educative or that is conducive to growth. There is no subject that is in and of itself, or without regard to the stage of growth attained by the learner, such that inherent educational value can be attributed to it. Failure to take into account adaptation to the needs and capacities of individuals was the source of the idea that certain subjects and certain methods are intrinsically cultural or intrinsically good for mental discipline. There is no such thing as educational value in the abstract. The notion that some subjects and methods and that acquaintance with certain facts and truths possess educational value in and of themselves is the reason why traditional education reduced the material of education so largely to a diet of predigested materials. According to this notion, it was enough to regulate the quantity and difficulty of the material provided, in a scheme of quantitative grading, from month to month and from year to year. Otherwise a pupil was expected to take it in the doses that were prescribed from without. If the pupil left it instead of taking it, if he engaged in physical truancy, or in the mental truancy of mind-wandering and finally built up an emotional revulsion against the subject, he was held to be at fault. No question was raised as to whether the trouble might not lie in the subject-matter or in the way in which it was offered. The principle of interaction makes it clear that failure of adaptation of material to needs and capacities of individuals may cause an experience to be non-educative quite as much as failure of an individual to adapt himself to the material.

The principle of continuity in its educational application means, nevertheless, that the future has to be taken into account at every stage of the educational process. This idea is easily misunderstood and is badly distorted in traditional education. Its assumption is, that by acquiring certain skills and by learning certain subjects which would be needed later (perhaps in college or perhaps in adult life) pupils are as a matter of course made ready for the needs and circumstances of the future. Now "preparation" is a treacherous idea. In a certain sense every experience should do something to prepare a person for later experiences of a deeper and more expansive quality. That is the very meaning of growth, continuity, reconstruction of experience. But it is a mistake to suppose that the mere acquisition of a certain amount of arithmetic, geography, history, etc., which is taught and studied because it may be useful at some time in the future, has this effect, and it is a mistake to suppose that acquisition of skills in reading and figuring will automatically constitute preparation for their right and effective use under conditions very unlike those in which they were acquired.

Almost everyone has had occasion to look back upon his school days and wonder what has become of the knowledge he was supposed to have amassed during his years of schooling, and why it is that the technical skills he acquired have to be learned over again in changed form in order to stand him in good stead. Indeed, he is lucky who does not find that in order to make progress, in order to go ahead intellectually, he does not have to unlearn much of what he learned in school. These questions cannot be disposed of by saying that the subjects were not actually learned, for they were learned at least sufficiently to enable a pupil to pass examinations in them. One trouble is that the subject-matter in question was learned in isolation; it was put, as it were, in a watertight compartment. When the question is asked, then, what has become of it, where has it gone to, the right answer is that it is still there in the special compartment in which it was originally stowed away. If exactly the same conditions recurred as those under which it was acquired, it would also recur and be available. But it was segregated when it was acquired and hence is so disconnected from the rest of experience that it is not available under the actual conditions of life. It is contrary to the laws of experience that learning of this kind, no matter how thoroughly engrained at the time, should give genuine preparation.

Nor does failure in preparation end at this point. Perhaps the greatest of all pedagogical fallacies is the notion that a person learns only the particular thing he is studying at the time. Collateral learning in the way of formation of enduring attitudes, of likes and dislikes, may be and often is much more important than the spelling lesson or lesson in geography or history that is learned. For these attitudes are fundamentally what count in the future. The most important attitude that can be formed is that of desire to go on learning. If impetus in this direction is weakened instead of being intensified, something much more than mere lack of preparation takes place. The pupil is actually robbed of native capacities which otherwise would enable him to cope with the circumstances that he meets in the course of his life. We often see persons who have had little schooling and in whose case the absence of set schooling proves to be a positive asset. They have at least retained their native common sense and power of judgment, and its exercise in the actual conditions of living has given them the precious gift of ability to learn from the experiences they have. What avail is it to win prescribed amounts of information about geography and history, to win ability to read and write, if in the process the individual loses his own soul: loses his appreciation of things worth while, of the values to which these things are relative; if he loses desire to apply what he has learned and, above all, loses the ability to extract meaning from his future experiences as they occur?

What, then, is the true meaning of preparation in the educational scheme? In the first place, it means that a person, young or old, gets out of his present experience all that there is in it for him at the time in which he has it. When preparation is made the controlling end, then the potentialities of the present are sacrificed to a suppositious future. When this happens, the actual preparation for the future is missed or distorted. The ideal of using the present simply to get ready for the future contradicts itself. It omits, and even shuts out, the very conditions by which a person can be prepared for his future. We always live at the time we live and not at some other time, and only by extracting at each present time the full meaning of each present experience are we prepared for doing the same thing in the future. This is the only preparation which in the long run amounts to anything.

All this means that attentive care must be devoted to the conditions which give each present experience a worth-while meaning. Instead of inferring that it doesn't make much difference what the present experience is as long as it is enjoyed, the conclusion is the exact opposite. Here is another matter where it is easy to react from one extreme to the other. Because traditional schools tended to sacrifice the present to a remote and more or less unknown future, therefore it comes to be believed that the educator has little responsibility for the kind of present experiences the young undergo. But the relation of the present and the future is not an *Either-Or* affair. The present affects the future anyway. The persons who should have some idea of the connection between the two are those who have achieved maturity. Accordingly, upon them devolves the responsibility for instituting the conditions for the kind of present experience which has a favorable effect upon the future. Education as growth or maturity should be an ever-present process.

Questions

1. For Dewey, what are the two sides to education?
2. Is Dewey in favor of a child-centered curriculum? Explain.
3. In a time like ours, in which many homes and many families seem to be in disarray, would Dewey continue to argue that the school should exist on a continuum with the home? Explain.
4. Explain "reconstruction of experience."
5. If Dewey is right about reconstruction of experience, would you say that American schools today are trying to educate children? Explain.
6. What does Dewey mean in Article V of "My Pedagogic Creed"?
7. What is the difference between an aggregate and a community?
8. State "the democratic ideal" in your own words.
9. What is the relationship of democracy to education?
10. What are the two principles Dewey uses to evaluate experience?
11. How might you use those criteria in determining a curriculum or in determining how to treat your students?

Chapter 7

George S. Counts

TIME LINE FOR COUNTS

1889	Is born December 9 in Baldwin, Kansas.
1911	Receives A.B. from Baker University in Baldwin.
1913	Marries Lois H. Bailey. They have two children.
1916	Receives Ph.D. from University of Chicago. Begins teaching at Delaware College.
1919–1920	Is professor of secondary education at the University of Washington (in Seattle).
1920–1924	Is associate professor of secondary education at Yale.
1924–1926	Is professor of education at the University of Chicago.
1926	Publishes *Senior High School Curriculum*.
1927–1956	Is professor of education at Columbia University.
1929	Publishes *Secondary Education and Industrialism*.
1932	Publishes *Dare the School Build a New Social Order?*
1934	Publishes *Social Foundations of Education*.
1935	Receives the Teachers College Medal for Distinguished Service.
1938	Publishes *Prospects of American Democracy*.
1949	Publishes *Country of the Blind: The Soviet System of Mind Control*.
1955–1960	Serves as chairman of the Liberal Party of New York.
1957	Publishes *The Soviet Challenge to American Education*.

1959	Publishes *Khrushchev and the Central Committee Speak on Education.*
1963	Publishes *Education and the Foundation of Human Freedom.*
1974	Dies November 10.

Introduction

In many ways, George S. Counts's life and intellectual development mirror that of John Dewey. Both spent crucial early periods of their intellectual lives at the University of Chicago: Dewey taught there from 1895 to 1905 and developed many of his educational theories at the university's Lab School. Counts (1889–1974) missed Dewey's tenure at the University of Chicago, but did receive his doctorate from Chicago in 1916. Later both were faculty members at Columbia University and, in their writing and teaching, dramatically widened a traditional understanding of the university and the professorate. They were, in a sense, public intellectuals—thinkers who were willing to deal with contemporary issues not necessarily related to their field, thinkers who were able to deal with the interdisciplinary nature of the problems affecting contemporary life, and, perhaps most significantly, thinkers who viewed some form of action as the normal outgrowth of theory.

To understand Counts, it is useful to recall two salient biographical facts. First, Counts, a Kansas farm boy, was born into an era that, in effect, was disappearing: The great American frontier was closing. The dreams that constituted a previous America—of expansion, finding new lands, going West—were becoming less and less tenable. America, of geographic necessity, was closing in on itself and new dreams, new goals would have to be discovered if America was to retain the vitality that previously characterized it.

The second fact is more a function of Counts's time of maturity. As a young intellectual, coming of age in the teens and twenties, Counts was at once intrigued by the experiment that was taking place in the Soviet Union and dismayed by the apparent lack of moral purpose and seriousness exhibited in America at the time. As the Russians embarked on the great revolution of the twentieth century, Americans danced and drank their way through the party that was the roaring twenties. That party, of course, ended with the stock market crash of 1929.

The thirties, as much as they were a time of economic crisis, were times of spiritual and ethical distress. If the twenties were about acquiring material wealth and having a good time, what does a nation do when those goals are no longer reachable?

Throughout his career, Counts always considered himself a follower of John Dewey, and although Dewey himself was not always happy with that claim, there is reason to believe that Counts is one of the few philosophers of education who really took to heart Dewey's concluding remarks in Article V of "My Pedagogic Creed." There Dewey said "I believe that"

—the teacher is engaged, not simply in the training of individuals, but in the formation of the proper social life.

—every teacher should realize the dignity of his calling; that he is a social servant set apart for the maintenance of proper social order and the securing of the right social growth.

—in this way the teacher always is the prophet of the true God and the usherer in of the true kingdom of God.

Counts may be viewed as trying to work out the implications of those remarks, especially as those remarks were played out during what is arguably the worst crisis of American democracy in the twentieth century. When Counts's classic *Dare the School Build a New Social Order?* appeared in 1934, there was a widespread belief that something significant would have to be done or else the country would continue to drift aimlessly or find itself prey to a Soviet-style revolution. Counts, as the title of his work suggests, argued that the school should take the lead in creating a new and better social order. This meant, as the selections will show, a reexamination of the role of the teacher and an expansion of the notion of the educated person.

Counts's argument is almost classic in its simplicity. He starts with a claim of fact, to wit: Although some people might argue that education is about the simple transmission of information, a closer examination will show that education, in large part, is about the formation of character (remember Dewey's remarks quoted above). When teachers choose this text and not some other, when some teachers choose to focus on this part of the culture's legacy and not some other, when, using contemporary language, teachers choose to focus on Western culture as opposed to, say, Eastern or African, they are making choices that will have an impact on what their students think and feel, on what they value, and, ultimately, on what sorts of persons they will become. Thus, for Counts, education is fundamentally about imposition.

Now this imposition, assuming Counts is right in his factual claim, can be done in a number of different ways. First, and one might argue that this is the most typical way, it can be done in a blind and unintelligent fashion. The teacher is guided by all sorts of unstated or unknown assumptions. Some of those assumptions come from her or his own background (Is the teacher a liberal? a conservative? Does the teacher trust or fear children? and so on), some come from the board of education, some come from the other teachers, some come from the larger culture and the business community, and so on. Precisely because the imposition is done in a blind fashion, the possibility is always there that teachers will create "incoherent" characters—students operating with value systems that are seriously askew, that are fraught with contradictions.

Secondly, I think the imposition can be done in a conscious fashion where the goal is to replicate the dominant cultural and political ideology in the individual child. Here the teacher in effect, does a survey of the dominant cultural values, extracts them from their sources in the culture, and then, using her or his pedagogical skill and expertise, engenders the appropriate character in the student. For example, in the racist society, the racist teacher will consciously "stack" the curriculum, using, for example, literature, art, and statistical studies that support the racist position.

Finally, and this is Counts's main point, the imposition can be done in a conscious fashion with an eye toward improving the existing society. Paraphrasing Dewey, teachers should recognize the moral nature of the enterprise and use their skills to create a more just society.

Again, it is helpful to remember the context in which Counts worked. Counts and Dewey and virtually all American intellectuals who were raised in the latter part of the nineteenth century had an enormous faith in science as a tool for ensuring social progress. To use the language of postmodernism, nineteenth-century scholars viewed science as a "privileged narrative," a methodology that gave special insight into the nature of things and that could be used to solve human problems. Simply, Counts *assumed* that there was a way, a scientific way, to adjudicate disputes that to our contemporary ears seem questionable, namely How do you tell what a better society is? What criteria are used in deciding that issue and issues like it? and, perhaps most significantly, Who gets to decide the issue? For Counts, the significant question was exactly the one he asked. Should the schools (or somebody else) be in the business of creating a better society? For contemporary thinkers, there may be a question that takes precedence over Counts's: What *is* a better society?

This is not to say that *Dare the School Build a New Social Order?* is of mere antiquarian interest. In his classic work, Counts expands the notion of the educated person (or perhaps emphasizes a part of the notion that is frequently ignored) to include not merely information and skills but the quality of belief and the values and actions that flow from those beliefs. Just as Plato suggested that a truly knowledgeable person would be a good person, Counts suggests that an educated person would exhibit all sorts of ethical qualities. To divorce education, say, from the cultivation of democratic sentiments is to create, for Counts, a nation of technocrats, that is, an uneducated citizenry.

From *Dare the School Build a New Social Order?* (1932)

There is a fallacy that the school should be impartial in its emphases, that no bias should be given instruction. We have already observed how the individual is inevitably molded by the culture into which he is born. In the case of the

From *Dare the School Build a New Social Order?* by George S. Counts (Carbondale, IL: Southern Illinois University Press, 1932, copyright renewed 1959 by George S. Counts), pp. 16–18 and 50–52. Reprinted by permission of Martha L. Counts.

school a similar process operates and presumably is subject to a degree of conscious direction. My thesis is that complete impartiality is utterly impossible, that the school must shape attitudes, develop tastes, and even impose ideas. It is obvious that the whole of creation cannot be brought into the school. This means that some selection must be made of teachers, curricula, architecture, methods of teaching. And in the making of the selection the dice must always be weighted in favor of this or that. Here is a fundamental truth that cannot be brushed aside as irrelevant or unimportant; it constitutes the very essence of the matter under discussion. Nor can the reality be concealed beneath agreeable phrases. Professor Dewey states in his *Democracy and Education* that the school should provide a *purified* environment for the child. With this view I would certainly agree; probably no person reared in our society would favor the study of pornography in the schools. I am sure, however, that this means stacking the cards in favor of the particular systems of value which we may happen to possess. It is one of the truisms of the anthropologist that there are no maxims of purity on which all peoples would agree. Other vigorous opponents of imposition unblushingly advocate the "cultivation of democratic sentiments" in children or the promotion of child growth in the direction of "a better and richer life." The first represents definite acquiescence in imposition; the second, if it does not mean the same thing, means nothing. I believe firmly that democratic sentiments should be cultivated and that a better and richer life should be the outcome of education, but in neither case would I place responsibility on either God or the order of nature. I would merely contend that as educators we must make many choices involving the development of attitudes in boys and girls and that we should not be afraid to acknowledge the faith that is in us or mayhap the forces that compel us. . . .

As the possibilities in our society begin to dawn upon us, we are all, I think, growing increasingly weary of the brutalities, the stupidities, the hypocrisies, and the gross inanities of contemporary life. We have a haunting feeling that we were born for better things and that the nation itself is falling far short of its powers. The fact that other groups refuse to deal boldly and realistically with the present situation does not justify the teachers of the country in their customary policy of hesitation and equivocation. The times are literally crying for a new vision of American destiny. The teaching profession, or at least its progressive elements, should eagerly grasp the opportunity which the fates have placed in their hands.

Such a vision of what America might become in the industrial age I would introduce into our schools as the supreme imposition, but one to which our children are entitled—a priceless legacy which it should be the first concern of our profession to fashion and bequeath. The objection will of course be raised that this is asking teachers to assume unprecedented social responsibilities. But we live in difficult and dangerous times—times when precedents lose their significance. If we are content to remain where all is safe and quiet and serene, we shall dedicate ourselves, as teachers have commonly done in the past, to a role of futility, if not of positive social reaction. Neutrality with respect to the great issues that agitate society, while perhaps theoretically possible, is practically tantamount to giving support to the forces of conservatism. As Justice Holmes has candidly said in his essay on Natural Law, "we all, whether we know it or not, are fighting to make the kind of world that we should like." If neutrality is impossible even in the dispensation of justice, whose emblem is the blindfolded goddess, how is it to be achieved in education? To ask the question is to answer it.

To refuse to face the task of creating a vision of a future America immeasurably more just and noble and beautiful than the America of today is to evade the most crucial, difficult, and important educational task. Until we have assumed this responsibility we are scarcely justified in opposing and mocking the efforts of so-called patriotic societies to introduce into the schools a tradition which, though narrow and unenlightened, nevertheless represents an honest attempt to meet a profound social and educational need. Only when we have fashioned a finer and more authentic vision than they will we be fully justified in our opposition to their efforts. Only then will we have discharged the age-long obligation which the older generation owes to the younger and which no amount of sophistry can obscure. Only through such a legacy of spiritual values will our children be enabled to find their place in the world, be lifted out of the present morass of moral indifference, be liberated from the senseless struggle for material success, and be challenged to high endeavor and achievement. And only thus will we as a people put ourselves on the road to the expression of our peculiar genius and to the making of our special contribution to the cultural heritage of the race.

Questions

1. Do you think schools should "wage war on behalf of principles or ideals"? If so, which principles? Which ideals?
2. Counts claims to be "in agreement" with Dewey. Do you believe he is?
3. Should "democratic sentiments" be cultivated? If so, how would you go about such a cultivation?
4. Do you think schools (contemporary American ones) are in the business of imposing beliefs and values? Do you think the schools *should be* in the business of imposing beliefs and values? If so, which ones?
5. Is there a difference between indoctrination and education?
6. Would Counts say there is a difference between the two?
7. Counts makes a very strong case regarding the relationship of economics to education. Do you agree with him? Why or why not?
8. If Counts is right, how, for example, would you go about trying to educate one of your students who is homeless?

Chapter 8

Cornel West

TIME LINE FOR WEST

1953	Is born June 2 in Tulsa, Oklahoma. His father, a civilian air force administrator, his mother, an elementary school teacher, and his older brother and younger sisters moved frequently, finally settling down in Sacramento, California.
1970	Enrolls at Harvard University.
1973	Receives an A.B. degree.
1975	Receives an M.A. from Princeton University.
1975/6	Returns to Harvard as a Du Bois Fellow.
1980	Receives a Ph.D. from Princeton University.
1977–1984	Is assistant professor of philosophy and religion at Union Theological Seminary.
1979–1980	Serves as visiting professor at Yale University Divinity School.
1981	Serves as visiting professor at Barnard College, New York.
1982	Serves as visiting professor at Williams College, Williamstown, Massachusetts.
	Publishes *Prophecy Deliverance! An Afro-American Revolutionary Christianity*.
1983	Serves as visiting professor at Haverford College, Pennsylvania.
1984	Is appointed associate professor at Union Theological Seminary.

1984–1987	Is associate professor of philosophy and religion at Yale University.
1985	Publishes, with John Rajchman, an edited work, *Post-Analytic Philosophy*.
1987	Serves as visiting professor at University of Paris.
1988	Is named director of Afro-American studies at Princeton University. Publishes *Prophetic Fragments*.
1989	Publishes *The American Evasion of Philosophy: A Genealogy of Pragmatism*.
1991	Publishes *The Ethical Dimensions of Marxist Thought* and *Breaking Bread: Insurgent Black Intellectual Life*.
1993	Publishes *Race Matters; Keeping Faith; Prophetic Thought in Postmodern Times;* and *Prophetic Reflections: Notes on Race and Power in America*.
1995	Publishes, with Henry Louis Gates, *Colored People: A Memoir*.
1996	Publishes, with Henry Louis Gates, *The Future of the Race*.
1996	Publishes, with Michael A Lerner, *Jews and Blacks: A Dialogue on Race, Religion and Culture in America*.
1996	Publishes, with George E. Curry, *The Affirmative Action Debate*.
1998	Publishes, with Sylvia Ann Hewlett, *The War Against Parents: What We Can Do for America's Beleaguered Moms and Dads*.

Introduction

Cornel West is an enigma in a three-piece suit. Characterized by the *New York Times* as "a young, hip black man in an old, white academy; a believing Christian in a secular society; a progressive socialist in the age of triumphant capitalism; a cosmopolitan public intellectual among academic specialists," West defies easy classification.[1] Much like his characterization of Emerson, West refuses to "swim in a regulated pool nor allow others to imitate his stroke."[2] A professor of philosophy at Princeton, West has, in recent years, become more than just an academic celebrity. With his recent work *Race Matters* hovering on or near the best-seller list, West has become a public phenomenon.

Born in Tulsa, Oklahoma, West grew up in a working-class black area of Sacramento, California. According to his parents, young Cornel West set high standards for himself "academically, athletically, socially, and spiritually."[3] Very early in life he exhibited the ability to inspire others to focus on their best qualities and to overcome their weaknesses. While his personal accomplishments have been many—including acceptance at Harvard at age 16—West has remained a teacher (some might say a preacher), always using his intellectual prowess to assist others in making the most of themselves. Perhaps his greatest gift is his ability to live both in the "rarefied world of the mind"[4] and in the world of the oppressed African American, contributing to the transformation of both.

In short, West embodies his vision of the ideally educated individual. His ideally educated person, his prophetic thinker, is one who lives in and understands multiple realities and uses such understanding in building bridges between and among these varied worlds. Such an individual is fallible: No one has unmediated access to God, and progress toward creating a better world for humankind is in no way preordained or guaranteed. Though painfully aware of the bigotry and hatred that characterize much of our contemporary world, West refuses to abandon hope. It is at this point that West's spirituality emerges, manifesting itself in his faith that prophetic thinkers can make positive differences in our own and others' lives.

Long recognized as an outstanding scholar known for his critique of American religious and philosophic thought, West has more recently entered the public arena. In a recent work, published almost verbatim from his public lectures, West is clearly attempting to achieve a "public" voice. In this little book, *Prophetic Thought in Postmodern Times,* West explains for a general audience what he means by "prophetic thought." "There are," he suggests, "four basic components, four fundamental features, four constitutive elements."[5] These include discernment, connection, tracking hypocrisy, and hope.

Regarding discernment, West suggests that "prophetic thought must have the capacity to provide a deep and broad analytical grasp of the present in light of the past."[6] Such a deep understanding is necessary for grasping the complexities of the present and for conceptualizing possible visions of the future that build upon and extend the best that the past and present have to offer. In short, a prophetic thinker must be a bit of a historian, developing a vision of what should be out of a sophisticated understanding of what has been and is.

The second component of prophetic thought concerns the necessity of human connection. Here West suggests that a prophetic thinker must relate to or connect with others. Rather than just considering humankind in the abstract, prophetic thinkers must value and have empathy for fellow human beings. To West "empathy is the capacity to get in contact with the anxieties and frustrations of others."[7] Such empathy is in short supply in our modern world. Like William James before him, West agonizes over the all too common tendency of individuals today to treat others as stereotypical objects rather than as fellow beings worthy of respect.

To students, this failure to connect means that teachers just don't care. But many teachers do care and work very hard to help students. They are often "unable to make the connection that would complete caring relations with their students."[8] Their willingness to empathize with students is often thwarted by the dominant culture's desire to establish teaching "onto a firm scientific footing." As Noddings explains, both teachers and students have become victims in the search for the one best method of instruction. Both teachers and students have become "treatments" and "subjects" in the most recent manifestation of the science of pedagogy.

While the relationship between the need for empathy with others and pedagogy is fairly obvious, equally important for the prophetic thinker is the ability to identify and make known "the gap between principles and practice, between promise and performance, between rhetoric and reality." West identifies this third component of prophetic thought as a tracking of hypocrisy and suggests that it ought to be done in a self-critical rather than a self-righteous manner. It takes courage to boldly and defiantly point out human hypocrisy, but we must retain our humility by "remaining open to having others point out that of [our] own."9

West explains that a prophetic thinker cannot be one who has unmediated access to God. Such a view does not deny the necessity of faith for the prophetic thinker, but suggests that faith rests in humankind's ability to create better, more meaningful lives by learning from our mistakes. To participate in this component of prophetic thought is to be open to opinions different from our own. By considering other points of view, new evidence may emerge that refutes part or all of the original stance. In scrutinizing this new evidence it may prove to be inadequate or incorrect, thus enhancing the original position. In either case, knowledge has been expanded and progress made.

The fourth and perhaps most important component of prophetic thought is, simply, hope. West admits that, given the numerous and horrific examples of humankind's inhumanity to each other, it is hard to take hope seriously. Still, without it, all thought—including prophetic thought—is meaningless. As West explains,

> To talk about human hope is to engage in an audacious attempt to galvanize and energize, to inspire and to invigorate world-weary people. Because that is what we are. We are world-weary; we are tired. For some of us there are misanthropic skeletons hanging in our closet. And by misanthropic I mean the notion that we have given up on the capacity to do *anything* right. The capacity of human communities to solve any problem.10

West suggests that "we must face that skeleton as a challenge, not a conclusion." Even when confronted with numerous atrocities and multiple failures at creating community, the prophetic thinker must keep foremost in mind "the notion that history is incomplete, that the world is unfinished, that the future is open-ended and that what we think and what we do can make a difference."11 Without hope, in this sense, all that is left is sophisticated analysis resulting in a rather limited and largely meaningless life of the mind.

In the selection included here, taken from a public lecture titled "Beyond Multiculturalism and Eurocentrism," West illustrates the significance of each of these four components for confronting the crucial issues of our postmodern world. In a recent scholarly work, *Keeping Faith: Philosophy and Race in America*, West suggests that it takes all that is within him to remain hopeful about the "struggle for

114

human dignity and existential democracy." Noting "that not since the 1920s have so many black folk been disappointed and disillusioned with America," West admits that he shares these sentiments.[12] Still, in remaining true to the fourth component of prophetic thought, West refuses to abandon hope. West suggests that his branch of "prophetic pragmatism" offers a better way of illuminating and responding to contemporary crises. In short, West believes that the choice is clear for educators. As prophetic thinkers, and for our lives to have meaning, we must believe that what we think and do makes a difference.

Notes

1. An interview with Cornel West by Lucy Hodges, "Read, Hot and Black," *The Times Higher Education Supplement* vol. 1096 (November, 1993), p. 15.
2. Cornel West, *The American Evasion of Philosophy: A Genealogy of Pragmatism* (Madison: University of Wisconsin Press, 1989), p. 37.
3. Irene West and Clifton West, Foreword to Cornel West, *Prophetic Thought in Postmodern Times* (Monroe, ME: Common Courage Press, 1993), p. vii.
4. "Read, Hot and Black," p. 15.
5. West, *Prophetic Thought*, p. 3.
6. Ibid.
7. Ibid., p. 5.
8. Nel Noddings, *The Challenge to Care in Schools* (New York: Teachers College Press, 1993), p. 2.
9. West, *Prophetic Thought*, p. 5.
10. Ibid., p. 6.
11. Ibid.
12. Cornel West, *Keeping Faith: Philosophy and Race in America* (New York: Routledge, 1993), p. xvii.

From *Prophetic Thought in Postmodern Times* (1993)

. . . I am sure that most of you know that there has been a lot of talk about multiculturalism these days. It is a buzzword. It is often undefined. It tends to function in a rather promiscuous manner, to lie down with any perspective, any orientation. So we need to handle it. It is a rather elusive and amorphous term.

The same is true with Eurocentrism. What do we mean by Eurocentrism? Which particular European nation do you have in mind? Which classes of Europeans do you have in mind? Certainly, Sicilian peasants don't have the same status as Oxbridge elites. What Europe do you have in mind?

From *Prophetic Thought in Postmodern Times* by Cornel West (Monroe, ME: Common Courage Press ©. 1993 by Cornel West), pp. 7–21. Reprinted by permission of Common Courage Press, Box 702, Monroe, Maine, 04951.

We begin with the first moment of this lecture. There are three historical coordinates that will help us "situate and contextualize" this debate that is going on, as Brother John [Bolin who introduced this lecture series] puts it.

The Value of the Age of Europe

The first historical coordinate is the fact that we have yet to fully come to terms with the recognition that we live 48 years after the end of the Age of Europe. Between 1492 and 1945, powerful nations between the Ural mountains and the Atlantic Ocean began to shape the world in their own image. Breakthroughs in oceanic transportation, breakthroughs in agricultural production, breakthroughs in the consolidation of nation status, breakthroughs in urbanization, led toward a take-off.

1492, the problem of degrading other people and the expulsion of Jews and Muslims and wars in Spain. 1492, Christopher Columbus shows up in what to him is a New World. It is not new to indigenous peoples; they have been there for thousands of years, two hundred nations, as those of you who are here tonight in Tulsa know quite intimately.

But the New World concept was part of an expansionism, keeping in mind our ambiguous legacies. We don't want to romanticize and we don't want to trivialize. There were structures of domination already here before the Europeans got here. The plight of indigenous women, for example. It doesn't mean that the wiping out of indigenous peoples by disease and conquest some-how gets European conquistadors off the hook. But it means that there was always, already, oppression. In new forms it was brought.

1492, publication of the first grammar book in Indo-European languages by Antonio de Nebrija in Spanish. Language, of course, being the benchmark in the foundation of a culture. This is what is so interesting about multiculturalism these days. The fact that the dialogue takes place in English already says some-thing. For me, English is an imperial language. My wife is Ethiopian and she dreams in Amharic. I dream in English. That says something about us culturally. We still love each other, but it says something about us culturally. Namely, that I am part of a profoundly hybrid culture. I happen to speak the very language of the elite who tell me that I am not part of the human family, as David Walker said in his Appeal of September 1829. And she speaks Amharic, a different elite, in a different empire, an Ethiopian empire. Different hybridity. Different notions about what it means to be multicultural in this regard.

1492, a crucial year. Between 1492 and 1945, we see unprecedented levels of productivity. We see what, in my view, is the grand achievement of the Age of Europe. Because it was in some way marvelous, and it was in some other ways quite ugly. What was marvelous about it was the attempt to institutionalize cri-tiques of illegitimate forms of authority. Let me say that slowly: The attempt to hammer out not just critical gestures but critiques that could be sustained of arbitrary forms of power. That's what the Reformation was about in its critique of the Catholic Church.

Think what you will about Martin Luther. He was bringing critique to bear on what he perceived to be arbitrary forms of power. That is what the Enlightenment was about, fighting against national churches that had too much unaccountable power leading to too many lives crushed. That's what liberalism was about against absolute monarchy. That is what women's movements are about against male authority. That's what anti-racist movements are about against white supremacist authority.

They are building on traditions of critique and resistance. And, during the Age of Europe, given levels of productivity, there were grand experiments. Each and every one of them flawed, but grand experiments to try to live in large communities while institutionalizing critiques of illegitimate forms of authority. This was the makings of the democratic ideal, to which accountability to ordinary people became not just an abstract possibility, but realizable. As I say, it was deeply flawed.

The greatest experiment, as we know, began in 1776. But they were institutionalizing these critiques. It didn't apply to white men who had no property. It didn't apply to women. It didn't apply to slaves, people of African descent in the United States who were 21 percent of the population at that time. But that is not solely the point. It is in part the point. But it is not fully the point. The courageous attempt to build a democratic experiment in which the uniqueness of each and every one of us, the sanctity of each and every one of us who has been made equal in the eyes of God becomes at least possible.

That democratic idea is one of the grand contributions of the Age of Europe even given the imperial expansion, the colonial subjugation of Africa and Asia, the pernicious and vicious crimes against working people and people of color and so forth. So ambiguous legacy means, in talking about multiculturalism, we have got to keep two ideas in our minds at the same time. The achievements as well as the downfalls. The grand contributions and the vicious crimes.

The End of the Age of Europe and the Rise of the United States

1945. The Age of Europe is over. Europe is a devastated and divided continent. Mushroom clouds over Nagasaki and Hiroshima. Indescribable concentration camps in Germany. Again, Europe's inability to come to terms with the degradation of others. Now upon the hills of a divided continent emerges the first new nation. The U.S.A. Henry James called it a "hotel civilization." A hotel is a fusion between the market and the home. The home, a symbol of warmth and security, hearth. The market, dynamic, mobile, the quest for comfort and convenience. Both home and market. Deeply privatistic phenomenon. By privatistic, I mean being distant from, even distrustful of, the public interest and the common good.

In the first new nation, American civilization with tremendous difficulty was trying to define its national identity. What ought to be the common interest. What ought to be the common good. It is quite striking in fact that this first new nation doesn't even raise the question of what it means to be a citizen until after the Civil War, when they have to decide what is the status of the freed men and women, the ex-enslaved persons. The first new nation, a heterogenous population. People come from all around the world. In quest for what? Opportunity. In quest for what? A decent life. The quest for what? More comfort and convenience.

In 1945, we thought it would be—not "we," but Henry Luce did at least—the American Century. It only lasted 28 years. For the first time in human history, Americans created a modern social structure that looks like a diamond rather than a pyramid. Mass middle class, owing to the GI Bill, Federal Housing Administration programs, Workers' Compensation, Unemployment Compensation. The Great Society that played such a fundamental role in moving persons from working class to middle class in the United States. And yet, the distinctive feature of American civilization in its negative mode would be the institutionalizing of a discourse of whiteness and blackness.

The issue of race. Race is not a moral mistake of individuals, solely. It is a feature of institutions and structures that insures that one group of people have less access to resources, both material and intangible. By material, I mean money, housing, food, health care. By intangible, I mean things like self-confidence. I mean things like self-respect and self-regard and self-esteem. The discourse of whiteness and blackness would result in the incessant bombardment of people of color. Attacks on black beauty. Attacks on black intelligence. You can still get tenure in some universities for arguing that black people are not as intelligent as others. Where did that come from?

We are not concerned about eye color, not concerned about the shape of ears. But we are still concerned about pigmentation. It has a history. Of attacks on black intelligence. Attacks on black possibility. What is fascinating about this discourse, that in many ways is distinctive to the U.S.A., though South Africa shares it as well, is that those who came to the United States didn't realize they were white until they got here. They were told they were white. They had to learn they were white. An Irish peasant coming from British imperial abuse in Ireland during the potato famine in the 1840s arrives in the States. You ask him or her what they are. They say "I am Irish." No, you're white. "What do you mean I am white?" And they point me out. Oh, I see what you mean. This is a strange land.

Jews from Ukraine and Poland and Russia undergoing ugly pogroms, assaults and attacks, arrive in Ellis Island. They are told they have to choose, either white or black. They say neither, but they are perceived as white. They say I will not go with the goyim, the goyim have treated me like whites treat black people here. But, I am certainly not black either.

This is the 1880s. This is a time in which that peculiar American institution in which a black woman, a man, a child was swinging from a tree every two and a half days for thirty years. An institution unique to the United States called lynching, that "strange fruit that Southern trees bear" which Billy Holiday sang so powerfully about. It's happening every other day. And many Jews would say, no baby, I'm sure not identifying with these folk.

Arbitrary use of power. Unaccountable. Segregated laws, Jim and Jane Crow unaccountable. But yet, this new nation, after 1945, would emerge to the center of the historical stage. We now come to the third historical coordinate; the first was the end of the Age of Europe, the second was the emergence of the United States as a world power, and the third is the decolonization of the Third World.

The Decolonization of the Third World

By decolonization, I mean the quest of colonized people around the world, between 1945 and 1974, to break the back of European maritime empires. 1947, India. Exemplary anti-colonial struggle. Young preacher, 26 years old, Dexter Avenue Baptist Church, Montgomery, Alabama. He and courageous others look to India for anti-colonial strategy. Nonviolent struggle. Applies the same techniques and strategies to try to break the back of an apartheid-like rule of law in the United States.

The civil rights movement was part of a larger international attempt to bring critiques to bear on the empire building that had taken place during the heyday of the Age of Europe, namely the nineteenth century. '47 India, '49 China, '57 Ghana, '59 Cuba, '60 Guinea. We go on and on and on. '74 Angola. South Africa as yet to come. There is no way, of course, of looking past some of the colossal failures of the post-colonial regimes in some of those places, or the greed and corruption of the post-colonial elites, like Moi in Kenya, or Mengistu in Ethiopia, or Mobutu. The list is long.

But the decolonization points out the degree to which we are living in a fundamentally different world. In 1945, the U.N. had 45 nations; there are now 172 and there will be more soon given the disintegration of the Soviet Empire. It is a different world.

This is a way of situating broadly what the debate between multiculturalism and Eurocentrism is about. But it forces us to call into question anyone who would criticize Eurocentrism, as if, as I said before, it is monolithic. Because there are struggles going on in Europe between a whole host of different peoples with different cultures and different nations. And one has to begin with a nuanced historical sense in laying bare a genealogy or a history of the very term Europe itself.

Before the debate begins, when was Europe used for the first time as a noun? Christmas, 800, Charles the Great. Pope Leo III puts the crown upon his head. There's only Lombards and the Franks. Two out of eight clans. No Alamans. No Bavarians. An attempt to impose a unity from above. Arab caliphs threatening, Empress Irene in Greek Christendom. Unstable. Historians tell us that without Mohammed, Charlemagne would have been inconceivable. That is what Henri Pirenne says in his magisterial reading of this moment. And yet, at the same time, the attempt to conceive of Europe as some kind of homogenous entity collapses. 843. Partition. At Verdun. Territorial principalities. Their particularisms. Their multiplicities expand and surface. Europe as an entity is not taken seriously.

Second attempt, 1458. Pope Pius II, five years after the Turkish invasion of Constantinople. Responding to the Turkish menace, Europe is attempting to forge some collective identity. Reformation. Churches under national government, particularism again. Multiplicity again.

Last attempt made, 1804. Napoleon puts crown on his own head. And he calls himself not Emperor of Europe, but Emperor of France.

Francis II withdrew himself as Emperor, and said I am simply part of Austria now. After May, 1804, the collapse of Napoleon and we see the emergence of nationalism. A new tribalism in the human adventure. A nationalism that would strain the moral imagination. Populations around the world remain to this day in this central tribal division of humankind.

That is what is going on in Yugoslavia, that is what is going on in Russia. That is what is going on in Ethiopia between the Tigrans and the Amhara, and the Oromo. Nationalism. And this nationalism would dictate the rules of power during the heyday of the Age of Europe. So strong that people would be willing to die for it. That is pretty deep. That is pretty deep, that we all have to impose or endow some sense of meaning to our lives and one test is what we are willing to die for. And citizens around the world are willing to die for their nation-state. That's how deep the thread of nationalism is. That particular form of tribalism. And by calling it tribalism, I am not using that in a degrading sense. Because all of us are born under circumstances not of our own choosing, in particular families, clans, tribes and what-have-you. We all need protection. Tribes protect. Nation-states protect.

We all need identity. Tribes provide identity. But, of course, prophetic critique, and of course, in my view the Christian version of the prophetic critique, is that when any form of tribalism becomes a form of idolatry, then a critique and resistance must be brought to bear. When any form of tribalism becomes a justification for hiding and concealing social misery, critique and resistance must be brought to bear.

Economic & Social Decline

Let's come closer in our first moment of discernment. In our present moment here, and I will be saying more about this in the last lecture, but I want to touch on this now. From 1973 to 1989 was a period of national decline. For the first time since the '30s. Levels of productivity nearly freeze. A 0.4 percent increase in 1973–4.

There are reasons that we need not go into as to fragility of the debt structure linked to Third World nations. It has much to do, of course, with the rise of OPEC and the Third World monopoly of one of the crucial resources of the modern world, oil. We saw that in January [1991, during the Gulf War]. I think most of us are convinced that if the major resource of Kuwait was artichokes we would not have responded so quickly.

Which doesn't take away from the rhetoric of the liberation of Kuwait. Kuwaitis were, in fact, living under vicious and repressive regime under Sadaam Hussein. But there are a whole lot of regimes where people are living that we don't respond to. The rise of OPEC in '74 made a fundamental difference. The slowdown of the U.S. economy. No longer expanding. The unprecedented economic boom no longer in place. And since 1974, the real wages—by real wages I mean inflation-adjusted wages of non-supervisory workers in

America—have declined. Which means social slippage, which means downward mobility that produces fear.

Material uncertainty becomes real. As you can imagine, it serves as a raw ingredient for scapegoating. And from '73 to '89, we have seen much scapegoating. The major scapegoats have been women and black people, especially at the behest of certain wings of the Republican Party. We don't want to tar the Republican Party as a whole, but yes indeed, in '68 Nixon was talking about busing as a racially coded term. Harry Dent, the same architect of the strategy that led to the walkout of Strom Thurmond in 1948, due to the civil rights plank in the party, and the formation of the Dixiecrats. The same Harry Dent who served as the principal architect in '48 and lingered in '68.

Kevin Phillips wrote a book in '69 called *The New Republican Majority* which is an appeal to race to convince white working class ethnic workers that black people were receiving too much and were unjustified in what they were receiving and that whites were getting a raw deal and ought to come to the Republican Party.

Thomas and Mary Edsall tell the story in their recent *Chain Reaction*. The impact of rights and race and taxes on American politics. '76 the Democrats ride on the coattails of Watergate, but they have very little substance. In '80, Ronald Reagan consolidates it all and begins his campaign in Philadelphia, Mississippi and says state rights forever. Racially coded language. Political realignment. The Republican Party becomes essentially a lily-white party. Which is not to say that all Republicans are racist. It is a lily-white party.

Another feature is inadequate education for workers so that the products that they produce cannot compete. Japan, Taiwan and South Korea surge. Even Brazil. Stubborn incapacity to generate resources for the public square. No New Taxes, read my lips. Inability to generate resources means public squalor alongside private opulence.

The Ravages of the Culture of Consumption

Added to these problems is the undeniable cultural decay, which is in fact quite unprecedented in American history. This is what frightens me more than anything else. By unprecedented cultural decay I mean the social breakdown of the nurturing system for children. The inability to transmit meaning, value, purpose, dignity, decency to children.

I am not just talking about the one out of five children who live in poverty. I am not just talking about the one out of two black and two out of five brown children who live in poverty. I am talking about the state of their souls. The deracinated state of their souls. By deracinated I mean rootless. The denuded state of their souls. By denuded, I mean culturally naked. Not to have what is requisite in order to make it through life. Missing what's needed to navigate through the terrors and traumas of death and disease and despair and dread and disappointment. And thereby falling prey to a culture of consumption. A culture that promotes addiction to stimulation. A culture obsessed with bodily stimulation. A culture obsessed with consuming as the only way of preserving some vitality of a self.

You are feeling down, go to the mall. Feeling down, turn on the TV. The TV with its spectator passivity. You are receiving as a spectator, with no sense of agency, no sense of making a difference. You are observing the collapse of an empire and feeling unable to do anything about it, restricted to just listening to Dan Rather talk about it. A market culture that promotes a market morality.

A market morality has much to do with the unprecedented violence of our social fabric. The sense of being haunted every minute of our lives in our homes and on the street. Because a market morality puts money-making, buying and selling, or hedonistic self-indulgence at the center of one's behavior. Human life has little value. I want it, I want it now. Quick fix, I've got the gun, give it to me. It affects us all. I know some people try to run and move out to the suburbs and the technoburbs and so forth, but it affects us all. Market morality.

We should keep in mind that one of the great theorists of market society, namely Adam Smith, wrote a book in 1776, *The Wealth of Nations*. It is a powerful book in many ways. He talked about ways in which you generate wealth, but he also wrote a book in 1759 called *The Theory of Moral Sentiments*. And in that book Adam Smith argues that a market culture cannot sustain a market economy.

You need market forces as necessary conditions for the preservation of liberties in the economy. But when the market begins to hold sway in every sphere of a person's life, market conceptions of the self, market conceptions of time, you put a premium on distraction over attention, stimulation over concentration, then disintegration sets in. Also in this book, Adam Smith talks about the values of virtue and propriety, and especially the value of sympathy that he shared with his fellow Scot, David Hume. And when these nonmarket values lose influence or when their influence wanes, then you have got a situation of Hobbes' war of all against all, of cultural anarchy and social chaos.

Emile Durkheim put it another way, put it well when he said that a market culture evolves around a notion of contract, but every contractual relation presupposes precontractual commitments. So, a contract means nothing if there is no notion of truth telling and promise keeping. It has no status. It collapses. Now all we have is manipulative relations. I don't know how many of you have been reading Michael Levine's book, *The Money Culture*. I don't want to make an advertisement for it, but the book looks at what happens when a market culture begins to take over the center of a person's life. It tells stories about a Wall Street speculator who is upset because he only made 550 million dollars in a year. He has to make 555, and he is willing to take a risk and break the law to do it.

You say, what is going on? It cannot be solely a question of pointing fingers at individuals. We are talking about larger cultural tendencies that affect each and every one of us. It takes the form of self-destructive nihilism in poor communities, in very poor communities. The lived experience of meaninglessness and hopelessness and lovelessness. Of self-paralyzing pessimism among stable working-class and lower working-class people in which they feel as if their life, their standard of living is declining, they are convinced that the quality of life is declining. And yet, they are looking for quick solutions. I think in part that is what David Duke is all about. It is not just that the people who support him are racist, though, of course, many are. It's that they are looking for a quick solution to a downward slide they experience in their lives. He speaks to it in his own xenophobically coded language. The racist coded language. He is gaining ground.

There is a self-indulgent hedonism and self-serving cynicism for those at the top. To simply let it collapse and pull back. Public school, nothing to do with it. Public transportation, nothing to do with it. Public health, nothing to do with it. Privatize them because I have access to resources that allow me to privatize in such a way that I can have quality. The rest, do what you will, make it on your own.

In such a context, is it a surprise then, that we see tribal frenzy and xenophobic strife? Multiculturalism and Eurocentrism; two notions that go hand in hand. Our attempts on the one hand to respond to the tribal frenzy and xenophobic strife, and yet in their vulgar versions they contribute to it. These are highly unfortunate times which prepackage a debate resulting in even more polarization because it obscures and obfuscates what is fundamentally at stake in our moment. Intellectually, as I noted before, this means preserving the nuanced historical sense. But how do you preserve a historical sense in a market culture that effaces the past? A past that comes back to us through televisual means solely in the form of icons.

You go into any school today, who are the great figures? Martin Luther King, Jr. That is fine. Can you tell me something about the context that produced him. There is no King without a movement, there is movement without King. King is part of a tradition. But all we have is icons. George Washington. Icon. He was part of an armed revolutionary movement. He picked up guns and threw out the British imperialists. And he tried to institutionalize his conception of democracy. Grand but flawed, as I said before.

How do we preserve a sense of history in such a moment? What a challenge. But this is what is intellectually at stake. It makes no sense. Students read Toni Morrison and simply look in her text and see themselves rather than the challenge of a great artist who is dealing with collective memory and community breakdown in *Beloved*, for example. Challenge. If you look in a text and see yourself, that is market education, done in the name of education. But education must not be about a cathartic quest for identity. It must foster credible sensibilities for an active critical citizenry.

How do we preserve critical sensibility in a market culture? In our churches, in our synagogues, in our mosques, they are often simply marketing identity. It must be a rather thin identity, this market. It won't last long. Fashion, fad. Someone benefitting, usually the elites who do the marketing and benefitting. How deep does one's identity cut? Most importantly, what is the moral content of one's identity? What are the political consequences of one's identity? These are the kinds of questions that one must ask in talking about multiculturalism and Eurocentrism.

If one is talking about critiques of racism, critiques of patriarchy, critiques of homophobia, then simply call it that. Eurocentrism is not identical with racism. So, you deny the John Browns of the world. You deny the anti-racist movement in the heart of Europe. Eurocentrism is not the same as male supremacists. Why? Because every culture we know has been patriarchal in such an ugly way and that you deny the anti-patriarchal movements within the heart of Europe. And the same is so with homophobia. Demystify the categories in order to stay tuned to the complexity of the realities. That is what I am calling for. That is the role of prophetic thinkers and prophetic activists who are willing to build on discernment, human connection. Who are willing to hold up human hypocrisy, including their own, and also willing to hold up the possibility of human hope.

What I shall attempt to do tomorrow [in the second lecture] is to look at a distinctive American tradition that makes democracy its object of focus, its object of investigation, namely, American pragmatism. And pragmatism has nothing to do with practicalism or opportunism, which is the usual meaning of that term which you see in your newspapers. So and so was pragmatic. No principles, just did what had to be done. No, no. That is not what we will be talking about. American pragmatism is a distinct philosophical tradition that begins with Charles Sanders Peirce, through William James, through John Dewey, and Sidney Hook and W. E. B. Du Bois, all the way up to the present. And, it makes democracy a basic focus.

Its fundamental focus and question is, what are the prospects of democracy? How do you promote individuality and allow it to flower and flourish? I will be linking this tradition with the deep sense of the tragic, which I think the pragmatic tradition lacks. I will try to show ways in which Christian resources can be brought to bear to keep track of the sense of the tragic without curtailing agency. Without curtailing possibilities for action and then I will end [in the third lecture] with what the future of prophetic thought looks like. And I will try to answer some of those questions about whether indeed we can even talk about preserving a historical sense and subtle analysis in a culture that is so saturated by market sensibilities. Thank you so very much.

༄

Questions

1. What are the four basic components of "prophetic thought"?
2. How does West apply each of these components in his discussion of Eurocentrism and multiculturalism?
3. According to West, what was marvelous about the Age of Europe?
4. In terms of multiculturalism, why is the legacy of the Age of Europe ambiguous?
5. According to West, what are the pros and cons of tribalism?
6. Why does race matter so much in the cultures of the United States?
7. What are the chief characteristics of the cultural decay we are experiencing?
8. Why does this cultural decay frighten West more than anything else?
9. What does West mean by the phrase "public squalor alongside private opulence"?
10. In a society ravaged by a culture of consumption, how do we foster the development of prophetic thinkers?
11. In your own words, describe West's vision of the ideally educated individual.

Chapter 9

Paulo Freire

TIME LINE FOR FREIRE

1921	Is born in Recife, Brazil.
1959	Receives Ph.D. from University of Recife.
	Is named professor of philosophy and education.
1962	Is named director of the university's Cultural Extension Service.
	Begins a literacy program for peasants and workers.
1964	Is arrested and imprisoned (for seventy days). He is then forced into exile with his wife, Elza, and their five children.
	Travels from Brazil to Bolivia to Chile to Massachusetts and then to Switzerland.
1970	Works for the World Council of Churches in Geneva.
1972	Publishes *Pedagogy of the Oppressed*.
1974	Publishes *Education for Critical Consciousness*.
1976	Publishes *Educational Practice of Freedom*.
1980	Returns with his family to Brazil.
1985	Is appointed minister of education, Rio de Janeiro.
1986	Receives the UNESCO Prize for Education award.
1994	Publishes *Pedagogy of Hope*.
1996	Publishes *Letters to Cristina*.
1997	Publishes *Pedagogy of the Heart*.

| 1997 | Publishes *Teachers as Cultural Workers.* |
| 1997 | Dies. |

∾

Introduction

It can be said of Paulo Freire that he practices what he preaches. Freire offers us a utopian vision of what life should be and articulates a progressive pedagogy for attaining this desired goal. Though utopian, his democratic vision is grounded in the poverty and oppression that characterized his native area of Recife, Brazil. As Richard Shaull suggests in his foreword to *Pedagogy of the Oppressed,* "Freire's thought represents the response of a creative mind and sensitive conscience to the extraordinary misery and suffering of the oppressed around him."[1] Living in abject poverty as a child, Freire experienced and understood what he later named the "culture of silence" that characterizes the dispossessed. Victimized by the economic, social, and political paternalism of the dominant classes, the poor and dispossessed are not equipped, suggests Freire, to respond to the world's realities in a critical fashion. According to Freire, the dominant classes devised an educational system for the purpose of keeping the masses "submerged" and contained in a "culture of silence."

Perhaps because he shared the plight of the "wretched of the earth",—his family lost its middle-class status during the worldwide depression of the 1930s—Freire realized that the "culture of silence" could and should be overcome. Aware that the extant educational system fostered and sustained this culture of silence, Freire retained his faith in the power of a genuine education to enable and empower even the most wretched to first recognize their oppressed condition and then participate in its transformation. To assist those submerged in this culture of silence, Freire combined theory and practice into what is best known as a "pedagogy of the oppressed." It is important to note that this pedagogy did not emerge full-blown out of the mind of Freire but evolved as he worked with the dispossessed of his own country. In developing a pedagogy that centers on dialogue, that is, "the encounter between men, mediated by the world, in order to name the world," Freire remained true to his basic beliefs that all human beings merit our respect and are capable of understanding and transforming the world of which they are a part.

Experiencing firsthand the hunger and poverty that characterized Recife during the 1930s, Freire fell behind in school and was thought by some to be mentally retarded. Though he suffered no serious or permanent damage from his malnourishment, the experience affected him greatly. While still an adolescent, Freire devoted himself to working among the poor to assist them in improving their lot in life. This led to the study of law and to working as a labor union lawyer "among the people of the slums." In trying to help the poor understand their legal rights, Freire became involved in adult literacy programs during the late 1940s. Working with such programs for more than a decade, Freire rejected traditional methods of instruction, finding them much too authoritarian to be effective in teaching adults to read.

As he began doctoral study at the University of Recife, Freire read and made use of the insights of such great minds as "Sartre and Mounier, Eric Fromm and Lois Althusser, Ortega y Gassett and Mao, Martin Luther King and Che Guevara, Unamuno and Marcuse,"[2] but his educational philosophy remained grounded in these experiences of working with the dispossessed of Brazil. Though he first articulated his philosophy of education in his doctoral dissertation, Freire continued to advocate for a "problem-posing" approach to teaching as a member of the faculty of the University of Recife and of Harvard University.

In contrast to the "banking" method of education—where one privileged to know the truth deposits it in the appropriate amount and form into the empty and limited minds of the unwashed or dispossessed—Freire advocates an education or pedagogy that enhances and expands every human being's ability to understand and transform the world of which she or he is a part. For example, in teaching Brazilian peasants to read, Freire did not lecture to them. Instead, by beginning with a concept or concepts with which they were already familiar, Freire helped the peasants understand that they too were makers of culture and that they could contribute to the transformation of their own reality.

Beginning with a series of pictures "designed to demonstrate the fundamental differences between *nature* (the natural world) and *culture* (all that is created or transformed by men and women),"[3] Freire was able to assist illiterates in developing rudimentary literacy skills within thirty hours. As the peasants begin to learn the symbols for the words that name concepts familiar to them, their view of their world gradually expands. Through this process they begin to understand that "their world is not fixed and immutable," but is a reality in process that can be transformed.

Clearly, Freire's "pedagogy of the oppressed" is more than just literacy training. It is nothing less than a liberating process that enables and empowers each human being to achieve humankind's ontological vocation, that is, "to be a Subject who acts upon and transforms his world. . . ."[4] As human beings regain the right to rename their worlds, individually and collectively they consciously engage in the uniquely human activity of constructing and reconstructing their own worlds.

Though Freire's ideas are grounded in the poverty and oppression of his earlier years, the utility of his approach transcends national, class, and ethnic boundaries. According to Freire, the transforming power of words enables all of us to live fuller, more humane lives. As Peter J. Caulfield explains, "words," for Freire, "have meaning only in relation to their effect on human beings and the world in which we live." For example, the word *Chernobyl* connotes much more than merely a geographic location in what was once the Soviet Union. Many of us probably correctly associate the word with the worst nuclear accident in human history, but to appreciate the richness of such a statement, its many layers of meaning need to be connected to each person's personal reality. In short, for those who relate it to the dropping of atomic bombs during World War II and to the effects of radiation exposure produced by continued testing of nuclear weapons during the 1950s and 1960s, *Chernobyl* connotes more than it does for someone whose knowledge is limited to the accounts of the disaster provided by

127

the news media. From Freire's point of view, it is the educator's task to assist individuals in expanding the connection between concepts or issues of importance to them to a larger evolving reality. As Caulfield suggests:

> In order for students to comprehend truly the meaning of Chernobyl, they would probably need to discuss among themselves (with the teacher's help) the effects of radiation on neighboring grasses, vegetables, animals, and people, perhaps through generations. Indeed, how could they grasp the threat suggested by Chernobyl unless they researched Hiroshima and Nagasaki; they might also inquire into the long-term effects of radiation exposure to Americans living near atomic testing sites in Nevada in the 1950s. Only then would students begin to comprehend the significance of a statement like "Chernobyl was the site of the first serious nuclear accident."[5]

Such a progressive approach to pedagogy is a far cry from the "banking" education so prevalent in educational institutions throughout the world. In the selections that follow, Freire, in addition to critiquing such traditional pedagogies, explains his "problem-posing" approach to education.

Notes

1. Paulo Freire, *Pedagogy of the Oppressed* (New York: The Seabury Press, 1972), p. 10.
2. Ibid., p. 11.
3. Peter J. Caulfield, "From Brazil to Buncombe County: Freire and Posing Problems," *Educational Forum* 55:4 (Summer 1991), p. 312.
4. Freire, *Pedagogy of the Oppressed*, p. 12.
5. Caulfield, "From Brazil to Buncombe County," pp. 309–310.

From *Pedagogy of the Oppressed* (1972)

A careful analysis of the teacher-student relationship at any level, inside or outside the school, reveals its fundamentally *narrative* character. This relationship involves a narrating Subject (the teacher) and patient, listening objects (the students). The contents, whether values or empirical dimensions of reality, tend in the process of being narrated to become lifeless and petrified. Education is suffering from narration sickness.

The teacher talks about reality as if it were motionless, static, compartmentalized, and predictable. Or else he expounds on a topic completely alien to the existential experience of the students. His task is to "fill" the students with the contents of his narration—contents which are detached from reality, disconnected

---

from the totality that engendered them and could give them significance. Words are emptied of their concreteness and become a hollow, alienated, and alienating verbosity.

The outstanding characteristic of this narrative education, then, is the sonority of words, not their transforming power. "Four times four is sixteen; the capital of Pará is Belém." The student records, memorizes, and repeats these phrases without perceiving what four times four really means, or realizing the true significance of "capital" in the affirmation "the capital of Pará is Belém," that is, what Belém means for Pará and what Pará means for Brazil.

Narration (with the teacher as narrator) leads the students to memorize mechanically the narrated content. Worse yet, it turns them into "containers," into "receptacles" to be "filled" by the teacher. The more completely he fills the receptacles, the better a teacher he is. The more meekly the receptacles permit themselves to be filled, the better students they are.

Education thus becomes an act of depositing, in which the students are the depositories and the teacher is the depositor. Instead of communicating, the teacher issues communiqués and makes deposits which the students patiently receive, memorize, and repeat. This is the "banking" concept of education, in which the scope of action allowed to the students extends only as far as receiving, filing, and storing the deposits. They do, it is true, have the opportunity to become collectors or cataloguers of the things they store. But in the last analysis, it is men themselves who are filed away through the lack of creativity, transformation, and knowledge in this (at best) misguided system. For apart from inquiry, apart from the praxis, men cannot be truly human. Knowledge emerges only through invention and re-invention, through the restless, impatient, continuing, hopeful inquiry men pursue in the world, with the world, and with each other.

In the banking concept of education, knowledge is a gift bestowed by those who consider themselves knowledgeable upon those whom they consider to know nothing. Projecting an absolute ignorance onto others, a characteristic of the ideology of oppression, negates education and knowledge as processes of inquiry. The teacher presents himself to his students as their necessary opposite; by considering their ignorance absolute, he justifies his own existence. The students, alienated like the slave in the Hegelian dialectic, accept their ignorance as justifying the teacher's existence—but, unlike the slave, they never discover that they educate the teacher.

The *raison d'être* of libertarian education, on the other hand, lies in its drive towards reconciliation. Education must begin with the solution of the teacher-student contradiction, by reconciling the poles of the contradiction so that both are simultaneously teachers *and* students.

This solution is not (nor can it be) found in the banking concept. On the contrary, banking education maintains and even stimulates the contradiction through the following attitudes and practices, which mirror oppressive society as a whole:

    a. the teacher teaches and the students are taught;

    b. the teacher knows everything and the students know nothing;

c. the teacher thinks and the students are thought about;

d. the teacher talks and the students listen—meekly;

e. the teacher disciplines and the students are disciplined;

f. the teacher chooses and enforces his choice, and the students comply;

g. the teacher acts and the students have the illusion of acting through the action of the teacher;

h. the teacher chooses the program content, and the students (who were not consulted) adapt to it;

i. the teacher confuses the authority of knowledge with his own professional authority, which he sets in opposition to the freedom of the students;

j. the teacher is the Subject of the learning process, while the pupils are mere objects.

It is not surprising that the banking concept of education regards men as adaptable, manageable beings. The more students work at storing the deposits entrusted to them, the less they develop the critical consciousness which would result from their intervention in the world as transformers of that world. The more completely they accept the passive role imposed on them, the more they tend simply to adapt to the world as it is and to the fragmented view of reality deposited in them.

The capability of banking education to minimize or annul the students' creative power and to stimulate their credulity serves the interests of the oppressors, who care neither to have the world revealed nor to see it transformed. The oppressors use their "humanitarianism" to preserve a profitable situation. Thus they react almost instinctively against any experiment in education which stimulates the critical faculties and is not content with a partial view of reality but always seeks out the ties which link one point to another and one problem to another.

Indeed, the interests of the oppressors lie in "changing the consciousness of the oppressed, not the situation which oppresses them";[1] for the more the oppressed can be led to adapt to that situation, the more easily they can be dominated. To achieve this end, the oppressors use the banking concept of education in conjunction with a paternalistic social action apparatus, within which the oppressed receive the euphemistic title of "welfare recipients." They are treated as individual cases, as marginal men who deviate from the general configuration of a "good, organized, and just" society. The oppressed are regarded as the pathology of the healthy society, which must therefore adjust these "incompetent and lazy" folk to its own patterns by changing their mentality. These marginals need to be "integrated," "incorporated" into the healthy society that they have "forsaken."

The truth is, however, that the oppressed are not "marginals," are not men living "outside" society. They have always been "inside"—inside the structure which made them "beings for others." The solution is not to "integrate" them into the structure of oppression, but to transform that structure so that they can

---

[1] Simone de Beauvoir, *La Pensée de Droite, Aujord'hui* (Paris); ST, *El Pensamiento político de la Derecha* (Buenos Aires, 1963), p. 34.

become "beings for themselves." Such transformation, of course, would undermine the oppressors' purposes; hence their utilization of the banking concept of education to avoid the threat of student *conscientização*.

The banking approach to adult education, for example, will never propose to students that they critically consider reality. It will deal instead with such vital questions as whether Roger gave green grass to the goat, and insist upon the importance of learning that, on the contrary, *Roger* gave green grass to the *rabbit*. The "humanism" of the banking approach masks the effort to turn men into automatons—the very negation of their ontological vocation to be more fully human.

Those who use the banking approach, knowingly or unknowingly (for there are innumerable well-intentioned bank-clerk teachers who do not realize that they are serving only to dehumanize), fail to perceive that the deposits themselves contain contradictions about reality. But, sooner or later, these contradictions may lead formerly passive students to turn against their domestication and the attempt to domesticate reality. They may discover through existential experience that their present way of life is irreconcilable with their vocation to become fully human. They may perceive through their relations with reality that reality is really a *process*, undergoing constant transformation. If men are searchers and their ontological vocation is humanization, sooner or later they may perceive the contradiction in which banking education seeks to maintain them, and then engage themselves in the struggle for their liberation.

But the humanist, revolutionary educator cannot wait for this possibility to materialize. From the outset, his efforts must coincide with those of the students to engage in critical thinking and the quest for mutual humanization. His efforts must be imbued with a profound trust in men and their creative power. To achieve this, he must be a partner of the students in his relations with them.

The banking concept does not admit to such partnership—and necessarily so. To resolve the teacher-student contradiction, to exchange the role of depositor, prescriber, domesticator, for the role of student among students would be to undermine the power of oppression and serve the cause of liberation.

Implicit in the banking concept is the assumption of a dichotomy between man and the world: man is merely *in* the world, not *with* the world or with others; man is spectator, not re-creator. In this view, man is not a conscious being *(corpo consciente)*; he is rather the possessor of *a* consciousness: an empty "mind" passively open to the reception of deposits of reality from the world outside. For example, my desk, my books, my coffee cup, all the objects before me—as bits of the world which surrounds me—would be "inside" me, exactly as I am inside my study right now. This view makes no distinction between being accessible to consciousness and entering consciousness. The distinction, however, is essential: the objects which surround me are simply accessible to my consciousness, not located within it. I am aware of them, but they are not inside me.

It follows logically from the banking notion of consciousness that the educator's role is to regulate the way the world "enters into" the students. His task is to organize a process which already occurs spontaneously, to "fill" the students by making deposits of information which he considers to constitute true knowledge.[2] And since men "receive" the world as passive entities, education should make them more passive still, and adapt them to the world. The educated man is the adapted man, because he is better "fit" for the world. Translated into practice, this concept is well suited to the purposes of the oppressors, whose tranquility rests on how well men fit the world the oppressors have created, and how little they question it.

The more completely the majority adapt to the purposes which the dominant minority prescribe for them (thereby depriving them of the right to their own purposes), the more easily the minority can continue to prescribe. The theory and practice of banking education serve this end quite efficiently. Verbalistic lessons, reading requirements,[3] the methods for evaluating "knowledge," the distance between the teacher and the taught, the criteria for promotion: everything in this ready-to-wear approach serves to obviate thinking.

The bank-clerk educator does not realize that there is no true security in his hypertrophied role, that one must seek to live *with* others in solidarity. One cannot impose oneself, nor even merely co-exist with one's students. Solidarity requires true communication, and the concept by which such an educator is guided fears and proscribes communication.

Yet only through communication can human life hold meaning. The teacher's thinking is authenticated only by the authenticity of the students' thinking. The teacher cannot think for his students, nor can he impose his thought on them. Authentic thinking, thinking that is concerned about *reality*, does not take place in ivory tower isolation, but only in communication. If it is true that thought has meaning only when generated by action upon the world, the subordination of students to teachers becomes impossible.

Because banking education begins with a false understanding of men as objects, it cannot promote the development of what Fromm calls "biophily," but instead produces its opposite: "necrophily."

> While life is characterized by growth in a structured, functional manner, the necrophilous person loves all that does not grow, all that is mechanical. The necrophilous person is driven by the desire to transform the organic into the inorganic, to approach life mechanically, as if all living persons were things. . . . Memory, rather than experience; having, rather than being, is what counts. The necrophilous person can relate to an object—a flower or a person—only if he possesses it; hence a threat to his possession is a threat to himself; if he loses possession he loses contact with the world. . . . He loves control, and in the act of controlling he kills life.[4]

---

[2] This concept corresponds to what Sartre calls the "digestive" or "nutritive" concept of education, in which knowledge is "fed" by the teacher to the students to "fill them out." See Jean-Paul Sartre, "Une idée fondamentale de la phénomenologie de Husserl: L'intentionalité," *Situations I* (Paris, 1947).

[3] For example, some professors specify in their reading lists that a book should be read from pages 10 to 15—and do this to "help" their students!

[4] Eric Fromm, *The Heart of Man* (New York 1966), p. 41.

Oppression—overwhelming control—is necrophilic; it is nourished by love of death, not life. The banking concept of education, which serves the interests of oppression, is also necrophilic. Based on a mechanistic, static, naturalistic, spatialized view of consciousness, it transforms students into receiving objects. It attempts to control thinking and action, leads men to adjust to the world, and inhibits their creative power.

When their efforts to act responsibly are frustrated, when they find themselves unable to use their faculties, men suffer. "This suffering due to impotence is rooted in the very fact that the human equilibrium has been disturbed."[5] But the inability to act which causes men's anguish also causes them to reject their impotence, by attempting

> . . . to restore [their] capacity to act. But can [they], and how? One way is to submit to and identify with a person or group having power. By this symbolic participation in another person's life, [men have] the illusion of acting, when in reality [they] only submit to and become a part of those who act.[6]

Populist manifestations perhaps best exemplify this type of behavior by the oppressed, who, by identifying with charismatic leaders, come to feel that they themselves are active and effective. The rebellion they express as they emerge in the historical process is motivated by that desire to act effectively. The dominant elites consider the remedy to be more domination and repression, carried out in the name of freedom, order, and social peace (that is, the peace of the elites). Thus they can condemn—logically, from their point of view—"the violence of a strike by workers and [can] call upon the state in the same breath to use violence in putting down the strike."[7]

Education as the exercise of domination stimulates the credulity of students, with the ideological intent (often not perceived by educators) of indoctrinating them to adapt to the world of oppression. This accusation is not made in the naïve hope that the dominant elites will thereby simply abandon the practice. Its objective is to call the attention of true humanists to the fact that they cannot use banking educational methods in the pursuit of liberation, for they would only negate that very pursuit. Nor may a revolutionary society inherit these methods from an oppressor society. The revolutionary society which practices banking education is either misguided or mistrusting of men. In either event, it is threatened by the specter of reaction.

Unfortunately, those who espouse the cause of liberation are themselves surrounded and influenced by the climate which generates the banking concept, and often do not perceive its true significance or its dehumanizing power. Paradoxically, then, they utilize this same instrument of alienation in what they consider an effort to liberate. Indeed, some "revolutionaries" brand as "innocents," "dreamers," or even "reactionaries" those who would challenge this

---

[5] Ibid., p. 31.

[6] Ibid.

[7] Reinhold Niebuhr, *Moral Man and Immoral Society* (New York, 1960), p. 130.

educational practice. But one does not liberate men by alienating them. Authentic liberation—the process of humanization—is not another deposit to be made in men. Liberation is a praxis: the action and reflection of men upon their world in order to transform it. Those truly committed to the cause of liberation can accept neither the mechanistic concept of consciousness as an empty vessel to be filled, nor the use of banking methods of domination (propaganda, slogans—deposits) in the name of liberation.

Those truly committed to liberation must reject the banking concept in its entirety, adopting instead a concept of men as conscious beings, and consciousness as consciousness intent upon the world. They must abandon the educational goal of deposit-making and replace it with the posing of the problems of men in their relations with the world. "Problem-posing" education, responding to the essence of consciousness—*intentionality*—rejects communiqués and embodies communication. It epitomizes the special characteristic of consciousness: being *conscious of,* not only as intent on objects but as turned in upon itself in a Jasperian "split"—consciousness as consciousness *of* consciousness.

Liberating education consists in acts of cognition, not transferrals of information. It is a learning situation in which the cognizable object (far from being the end of the cognitive act) intermediates the cognitive actors—teacher on the one hand and students on the other. Accordingly, the practice of problem-posing education entails at the outset that the teacher-student contradiction be resolved. Dialogical relations—indispensable to the capacity of cognitive actors to cooperate in perceiving the same cognizable object—are otherwise impossible.

Indeed, problem-posing education, which breaks with the vertical patterns characteristic of banking education, can fulfill its function as the practice of freedom only if it can overcome the above contradiction. Through dialogue, the teacher-of-the-students and the students-of-the-teacher cease to exist and a new term emerges: teacher-student with students-teachers. The teacher is no longer merely the-one-who-teaches, but one who is himself taught in dialogue with the students, who in turn while being taught also teach. They become jointly responsible for a process in which all grow. In this process, arguments based on "authority" are no longer valid; in order to function, authority must be *on the side of* freedom, not *against* it. Here, no one teaches another, nor is anyone self-taught. Men teach each other, mediated by the world, by the cognizable objects which in banking education are "owned" by the teacher.

The banking concept (with its tendency to dichotomize everything) distinguishes two stages in the action of the educator. During the first, he cognizes a cognizable object while he prepares his lessons in his study or his laboratory; during the second, he expounds to his students about that object. The students are not called upon to know, but to memorize the contents narrated by the teacher. Nor do the students practice any act of cognition, since the object towards which that act should be directed is the property of the teacher rather than a medium evoking the critical reflection of both teacher and students. Hence in the name of the "preservation of culture and knowledge" we have a system which achieves neither true knowledge nor true culture.

The problem-posing method does not dichotomize the activity of the teacher-student: he is not "cognitive" at one point and "narrative" at another. He is always "cognitive," whether preparing a project or engaging in dialogue with the students. He does not regard cognizable objects as his private property, but as the object of reflection by himself and the students. In this way, the problem-posing educator constantly re-forms his reflections in the reflection of the students. The students—no longer docile listeners—are now critical co-investigators in dialogue with the teacher. The teacher presents the material to the students for their consideration, and reconsiders his earlier considerations as the students express their own. The role of the problem-posing educator is to create, together with the students, the conditions under which knowledge at the level of the *doxa* is superseded by the true knowledge, at the level of the *logos*.

Whereas banking education anesthetizes and inhibits creative power, problem posing education involves a constant unveiling of reality. The former attempts to maintain the *submersion* of consciousness; the latter strives for the *emergence* of consciousness and *critical intervention* in reality.

Students, as they are increasingly posed with problems relating to themselves in the world and with the world, will feel increasingly challenged and obliged to respond to that challenge. Because they apprehend the challenge as interrelated to other problems within a total context, not as a theoretical question, the resulting comprehension tends to be increasingly critical and thus constantly less alienated. Their response to the challenge evokes new challenges, followed by new understandings; and gradually the students come to regard themselves as committed.

Education as the practice of freedom—as opposed to education as the practice of domination—denies that man is abstract, isolated, independent, and unattached to the world; it also denies that the world exists as a reality apart from men. Authentic reflection considers neither abstract man nor the world without men, but men in their relations with the world. In these relations consciousness and world are simultaneous; consciousness neither precedes the world nor follows it.

> La conscience et le monde sont dormés d'un même coup: extérieur par essence à la conscience, le monde est, par essence relatif à elle.[8]

In one of our culture circles in Chile, the group was discussing . . . the anthropological concept of culture. In the midst of the discussion, a peasant who by banking standards was completely ignorant said: "Now I see that without man there is no world." When the educator responded: "Let's say, for the sake of argument, that all the men on earth were to die, but that the earth itself remained, together with trees, birds, animals, rivers, seas, the stars . . . wouldn't all this be a world?" "Oh no," the peasant replied emphatically. "There would be no one to say: 'This is a world.'"

The peasant wished to express the idea that there would be lacking the consciousness of the world which necessarily implies the world of consciousness. *I* cannot exist without a *not-I*. In turn, the *not-I* depends on that existence. The

---

[8] Sartre, *Une idée fundamentale*, p. 32.

world which brings consciousness into existence becomes the world *of* that consciousness. Hence, the previously cited affirmation of Sartre: *"La conscience et le monde sont dormés d'un même coup."*

As men, simultaneously reflecting on themselves and on the world, increase the scope of their perception, they begin to direct their observations towards previously inconspicuous phenomena:

> In perception properly so-called, as an explicit awareness [*Gewahren*], I am turned towards the object, to the paper, for instance. I apprehend it as being this here and now. The apprehension is a singling out, every object having a background in experience. Around and about the paper lie books, pencils, ink-well, and so forth, and these in a certain sense are also "perceived," perceptually there, in the "field of intuition"; but whilst I was turned towards the paper there was no turning in their direction, nor any apprehending of them, not even in a secondary sense. They appeared and yet were not singled out, were not posited on their own account. Every perception of a thing has such a zone of background intuitions or background awareness, if "intuiting" already includes the state of being turned towards, and this also is "conscious experience," or more briefly a "consciousness of" all indeed that in point of fact lies in the co-perceived objective background.[9]

That which had existed objectively but had not been perceived in its deeper implications (if indeed it was perceived at all) begins to "stand out," assuming the character of a problem and therefore of challenge. Thus, men begin to single out elements from their "background awarenesses" and to reflect upon them. These elements are now objects of men's consideration, and, as such, objects of their action and cognition.

In problem-posing education, men develop their power to perceive critically *the way they exist* in the world *with which* and *in which* they find themselves; they come to see the world not as a static reality, but as a reality in process, in transformation. Although the dialectical relations of men with the world exist independently of how these relations are perceived (or whether or not they are perceived at all), it is also true that the form of action men adopt is to a large extent a function of how they perceive themselves in the world. Hence, the teacher-student and the students-teachers reflect simultaneously on themselves and the world without dichotomizing this reflection from action, and thus establish an authentic form of thought and action.

Once again, the two educational concepts and practices under analysis come into conflict. Banking education (for obvious reasons) attempts, by mythicizing reality, to conceal certain facts which explain the way men exist in the world; problem-posing education sets itself the task of demythologizing. Banking education resists dialogue; problem-posing education regards dialogue as indispensable to the act of cognition which unveils reality. Banking education

---

[9] Edmund Husserl, *Ideas—General Introduction to Pure Phenomenology* (London, 1969), pp. 105–106.

treats students as objects of assistance; problem-posing education makes them critical thinkers. Banking education inhibits creativity and domesticates (although it cannot completely destroy) the *intentionality* of consciousness by isolating consciousness from the world, thereby denying men their ontological and historical vocation of becoming more fully human. Problem-posing education bases itself on creativity and stimulates true reflection and action upon reality, thereby responding to the vocation of men as beings who are authentic only when engaged in inquiry and creative transformation. In sum: banking theory and practice, as immobilizing and fixating forces, fail to acknowledge men as historical beings; problem-posing theory and practice take man's historicity as their starting point.

Problem-posing education affirms men as beings in the process of *becoming*—as unfinished, uncompleted beings in and with a likewise unfinished reality. Indeed, in contrast to other animals who are unfinished, but not historical, men know themselves to be unfinished; they are aware of their incompletion. In this incompletion and this awareness lie the very roots of education as an exclusively human manifestation. The unfinished character of men and the transformational character of reality necessitate that education be an ongoing activity.

Education is thus constantly remade in the praxis. In order to *be*, it must *become*. Its "duration" (in the Bergsonian meaning of the word) is found in the interplay of the opposites *permanence* and *change*. The banking method emphasizes permanence and becomes reactionary; problem-posing education—which accepts neither a "well-behaved" present nor a predetermined future—roots itself in the dynamic present and becomes revolutionary.

Problem-posing education is revolutionary futurity. Hence, it is prophetic (and, as such, hopeful). Hence, it corresponds to the historical nature of man. Hence, it affirms men as beings who transcend themselves, who move forward and look ahead, for whom immobility represents a fatal threat, for whom looking at the past must only be a means of understanding more clearly what and who they are so that they can more wisely build the future. Hence, it identifies with the movement which engages men as beings aware of their incompletion—an historical movement which has its point of departure, its Subjects and its objective.

The point of departure of the movement lies in men themselves. But since men do not exist apart from the world, apart from reality, the movement must begin with the men-world relationship. Accordingly, the point of departure must always be with men in the "here and now," which constitutes the situation within which they are submerged, from which they emerge, and in which they intervene. Only by starting from this situation—which determines their perception of it—can they begin to move. To do this authentically they must perceive their state not as fated and unalterable, but merely as limiting—and therefore challenging.

Whereas the banking method directly or indirectly reinforces men's fatalistic perception of their situation, the problem-posing method presents this very situation to them as a problem. As the situation becomes the object of their cognition, the naïve or magical perception which produced their fatalism gives way to perception which is able to perceive itself even as it perceives reality, and can thus be critically objective about that reality.

A deepened consciousness of their situation leads men to apprehend that situation as an historical reality susceptible of transformation. Resignation gives way to the drive for transformation and inquiry, over which men feel themselves to be in control. If men, as historical beings necessarily engaged with other men in a movement of inquiry, did not control that movement, it would be (and is) a violation of men's humanity. Any situation in which some men prevent others from engaging in the process of inquiry is one of violence. The means used are not important; to alienate men from their own decision-making is to change them into objects.

This movement of inquiry must be directed towards humanization—man's historical vocation. The pursuit of full humanity, however, cannot be carried out in isolation or individualism, but only in fellowship and solidarity; therefore it cannot unfold in the antagonistic relations between oppressors and oppressed. No one can be authentically human while he prevents others from being so. Attempting *to be more* human, individualistically, leads to *having more*, egotistically: a form of dehumanization. Not that it is not fundamental *to have* in order *to be* human. Precisely because it *is* necessary, some men's *having* must not be allowed to constitute an obstacle to others' *having*, must not consolidate the power of the former to crush the latter.

Problem-posing education, as a humanist and liberating praxis, posits as fundamental that men subjected to domination must fight for their emancipation. To that end, it enables teachers and students to become Subjects of the educational process by overcoming authoritarianism and an alienating intellectualism; it also enables men to overcome their false perception of reality. The world—no longer something to be described with deceptive words—becomes the object of that transforming action by men which results in their humanization.

Problem-posing education does not and cannot serve the interests of the oppressor. No oppressive order could permit the oppressed to begin to question: Why? While only a revolutionary society can carry out this education in systematic terms, the revolutionary leaders need not take full power before they can employ the method. In the revolutionary process, the leaders cannot utilize the banking method as an interim measure, justified on grounds of expediency, with the intention of *later* behaving in a genuinely revolutionary fashion. They must be revolutionary—that is to say, dialogical—from the outset.

From *Letters to Cristina* (1996)

Second Letter

The piano in our house was like the tie around my father's neck. In spite of all our difficulties, we did not get rid of the piano, nor did my father do away with his necktie.

From *Letters to Cristina* by Paulo Freire (N.Y.: Routledge, 1996), pp. 21–24. Reprinted by permission of Routledge.

Born into a middle-class family that suffered the impact of the economic crisis of 1929, we became "connective kids." We participated in the world of those who ate well, even though we had very little to eat ourselves, and in the world of kids from very poor neighborhoods on the outskirts of town.[1]

We were linked to the former by our middle-class position; we were connected to the latter by our hunger, even though our hardships were less than theirs.

In my constant attempt to recollect my childhood, I remember that—in spite of the hunger that gave us solidarity with the children from the poor outskirts of town, in spite of the bond that united us in our search for ways to survive—our playtime, as far as the poor children were concerned, marked us as people from another world who happened to fall accidentally into their world.

Such class borders, which the man of today so clearly understands when he revisits his past, were not understood by the child of yesterday. Those borders were expressed more clearly by some of our friends' parents. Immersed in the alienating day-to-day routine, not understanding the causes behind the circumstances in which they were involved, the parents of these children were, by and large, existentially tired men and women who were historically anesthetized.

I cannot resist the temptation of making a parenthetical comment in this letter, calling attention to the relationship between class violence, class exploitation, existential tiredness, and historical anesthesia; that is, the fatalism among dominated and violated people before a world that is considered immutable. For this reason, the moment such people commit themselves to their political struggle, they begin to assert their position as a class. They transcend the fatalism that had anesthetized them historically. Such fatalism caused the parents of our poor friends to look at us as if they were thanking us for being friends with their sons and daughters. As if we and our parents were doing them a favor. To them, we were the sons of Captain Temístocles, we lived in a house in another section of the city; and our house was not like their huts in the woods.

---

[1] At the end of the past century and the beginning of this one, when the newly liberated slaves were settling themselves in the biggest and most important Brazilian cities, they evidently occupied the areas despised by the middle class and local elites. The narrow paths between the mountains and hills have been their leftovers ever since.

The narrow paths were no more than what many continue to be: gutters in which filthy, polluted, green water passed through. In them, even clean rain water turned to sludge due to trash, including that from the sewers. The imprudent children spent their leisure time swimming these waters before they reached the ocean and rivers. On its fetid banks, in areas prone to floods, the very poor built and continue to build their houses.

The residences in the hills do not present more comfort than those located on the banks of the narrow paths. The inhabitants have to descend and climb the slopes on foot, and if their houses are spared floods, the strong winds and torrential rains of the tropical zone can easily destroy them.

The mocambos endure the damage of inclemency better than the residences built with urban debris. The houses of the hills and narrow paths are without running water, electricity, sewage, or garbage collection.

In this manner, when Freire speaks of the "world of the kids who were from very poor neighborhoods on the outskirts of town" he is speaking about the excluded children, the children of the mocambos and of the hills. They are excluded from eating, attending school, being clothed properly, sleeping well, taking baths in clean water, and waiting for better days.

In our house, we had a German piano on which Lourdes, one of our aunts, played Chopin, Beethoven, and Mozart. The piano alone was enough to distinguish our class from that of Dourado, Reginaldo, Baixa, Toinho Morango, and Gerson Macaco, who were our friends in those days. The piano in our house was like the tie around my father's neck. In spite of all our difficulties, we did not get rid of the piano, nor did my father do away with his necktie. Both the piano and the necktie were, in the end, symbols that helped us remain in the class to which we belonged. They implied a certain lifestyle, a certain way of being, a certain way of speaking, a certain way of walking, a special way of greeting people that involved bowing slightly and tipping your hat, as I had often seen my father do. All of these things were an expression of class. All of these things were defended by our family as an indispensable condition of survival.

The piano was not a mere instrument for Lourdes's artistic enjoyment, nor were my father's neckties just a clothing style. They both marked our class position. To lose those class markers would have meant losing our solidarity with members of the middle class in a step-by-step march toward the poor people on the outskirts of town. From there it would have been very difficult to return to our middle-class milieu. It therefore became necessary to preserve those class markers in order psychologically to enable our family to deal with our financial crisis and maintain our class position.

Lourdes's piano and my father's neckties made our hunger appear accidental. With those markers, we were able to borrow money. Even though it was not easy, without them, it would have been almost impossible. With those markers, our childhood fruit thefts, if discovered, would have been treated as mere pranks. At most, they would have been a minor embarrassment for our parents. Without them, they would certainly have been characterized as child delinquency.

Lourdes's piano and my father's neckties played the same class role that the tropical jacaranda trees and fine china play today among Northeast Brazil's aristocracy, who are in decline. Perhaps aristocratic class markers are less effective today than Lourdes's piano and my father's neckties were during the 1930s.

I highlight the issue of social class because the dominant class insists, in eloquent discourses full of deceit, that what is important is not class, but the courage to work and be disciplined, and the desire to climb and grow. Therefore, those who triumph are those who work hard without complaining and are disciplined; that is, those who do not create problems for their masters.

It is for this reason that I have emphasized our origin and class position, explaining the gimmicks that our family developed in order to transcend our economic crisis.

I will never forget one of our gimmicks. It was a Sunday morning. Perhaps it was ten or eleven o'clock. It doesn't matter. We had just teased our stomachs with a cup of coffee and a thin slice of bread without butter. This would not have been enough food to keep us going, even if we had eaten plenty the day before, which we hadn't.

I don't remember what we were doing, if we were conversing or playing. I just remember that my two older brothers and I were sitting on the ledge of the cement patio at the edge of the yard where we lived. The yard contained some flower beds—roses, violets, and daisies—and some lettuce, tomatoes, and kale plants that my mother had pragmatically planted. The lettuce, tomatoes, and kale improved our diet. The roses, violets, and daisies decorated the living room in a vase that was a family relic from the last century. (Of these relics, my sister Stela still has the porcelain sink that was used to give us our first baths upon arriving in the world. Our sons and daughters were also bathed in the same porcelain sink. Regretfully, our grandchildren have broken with this family tradition.)

It was then that our attention was attracted by the presence of a chicken that probably belonged to our next-door neighbors. While looking for grasshoppers in the grass, the chicken ran back and forth, left to right, following the movements of the grasshoppers as they tried to survive. In one of those runs, the chicken came too close to us. In a split second, as if we had rehearsed it, premeditated it, we had the kicking chicken in our hands.

My mother arrived shortly after. She did not ask any questions. The four of us looked at each other and at the dead chicken in one of our hands.

Today, many years after that morning, I can appreciate the conflict that my mother, who was a Christian Catholic, must have felt as she looked at us in perplexity and silence. Her alternatives were either to reproach us severely and make us return the still warm chicken to our neighbors or to prepare the fowl as a special dinner. Her common sense won. Still silent, she took the chicken, walked across the patio, entered the kitchen, and lost herself in doing a job she had not done in a long time.

Our dinner that Sunday took place some hours later without any exchange of words. It is possible that we were tasting some remorse among the spices that seasoned our neighbor's chicken. The dish killed our hunger, yet the chicken was an accusatory "presence" that reminded us of the sin, the crime against private property, that we had committed.

The next day, our neighbor, upon noticing the loss of his chicken from the pen, must have cursed the thieves who could only have been the "little people," poor lower-class people, the kind who steal chickens.[2] He would never have imagined that the authors of the theft were close, very close to him indeed. Lourdes's piano and my father's neckties made any other conjecture impossible.

---

[2] Chicken thief was the name used in Northeast Brazil, before the violence of burglars had reached its cities, for those who committed small thefts to survive, having no job due to a sluggish economy.

The term indicated a thief who stole, almost accidentally, things he found in the backyards of the well-to-do—clothes, fruit, or even chickens.

"Little people" is the Brazilian term that arrogant middle-class and upper-class people call, even today, people deprived of material goods. Besides being discriminatory, the term is intended to hurt the individual, and rob him or her of the dignity of belonging.

It is as if being poor or miserable was disgraceful and worked against possessing moral or ethical qualities because of a nonprivileged social status. Therefore, "little people," men or women, were considered inferior individuals to whom we ought not give any respect or esteem. This term is highly pejorative, [and] therefore, Freire uses it in quotes.

Questions

1. What is a "culture of silence"?
2. How has our traditional education system submerged the masses in a "culture of silence"?
3. How did Freire develop a pedagogy of the oppressed?
4. Explain Freire's assertion that "education is suffering from narration sickness."
5. What is the "banking" concept of education?
6. What does Freire mean by the phrase "humankind's ontological vocation"?
7. How does this view of humankind differ from the perspective of humankind associated with "banking" education?
8. How do "bank-clerk" teachers dehumanize themselves and their students?
9. What is the difference between being *in* the world rather than *with* the world?
10. What does Freire mean by praxis?
11. Describe in your own words the problem-posing education advocated by Freire.
12. What role does dialogue play in problem-posing education?
13. If one embraces teaching as a problem-posing activity, what does one teach? What is the curriculum? Where does one begin?
14. What is humanization and why is this a goal worthy of Freire's pedagogy?
15. How might economic class determine classroom practice?
16. In your own words, describe the ideally educated individual from Freire's point of view.